CRISIS IN THE CENTRAL AFRICAN REPUBLIC

HEARING

BEFORE THE

SUBCOMMITTEE ON AFRICA, GLOBAL HEALTH, GLOBAL HUMAN RIGHTS, AND INTERNATIONAL ORGANIZATIONS

OF THE

COMMITTEE ON FOREIGN AFFAIRS HOUSE OF REPRESENTATIVES

ONE HUNDRED THIRTEENTH CONGRESS

FIRST SESSION

_____

NOVEMBER 19, 2013

_____

Serial No. 113–118

_____

Printed for the use of the Committee on Foreign Affairs

Available via the World Wide Web: http://www.foreignaffairs.house.gov/ or http://www.gpo.gov/fdsys/

_____

U.S. GOVERNMENT PRINTING OFFICE

85–638PDF   WASHINGTON : 2014

For sale by the Superintendent of Documents, U.S. Government Printing Office
Internet: bookstore.gpo.gov   Phone: toll free (866) 512–1800; DC area (202) 512–1800
Fax: (202) 512–2104   Mail: Stop IDCC, Washington, DC 20402–0001

CONTENTS

Page

WITNESSES

The Honorable Robert P. Jackson, Principal Deputy Assistant Secretary, Bureau of African Affairs, U.S. Department of State 4

The Most Reverend Nestor-Désiré Nongo-Aziagbia, Roman Catholic Bishop of Bossangoa, Central African Republic 20

Mr. Mike Jobbins, senior programme manager, Africa, Search for Common Ground 28

Mr. Philippe Bolopion, United Nations director, Human Rights Watch 37

LETTERS, STATEMENTS, ETC., SUBMITTED FOR THE HEARING

The Honorable Robert P. Jackson: Prepared statement 7

The Most Reverend Nestor-Désiré Nongo-Aziagbia: Prepared statement 23

Mr. Mike Jobbins: Prepared statement 31

Mr. Philippe Bolopion: Prepared statement 40

APPENDIX

Hearing notice.. 66

Hearing minutes 67

The Honorable Christopher H. Smith, a Representative in Congress from the State of New Jersey, and chairman, Subcommittee on Africa, Global Health, Global Human Rights, and International Organizations: The Central African Republic (CAR) fact sheet from the United States Commission on International Religious Freedom 68

The Honorable Edward R. Royce, a Representative in Congress from the State of California, and chairman, Committee on Foreign Affairs: Letter to the Honorable John F. Kerry, Secretary of State 73

CRISIS IN THE CENTRAL AFRICAN REPUBLIC

TUESDAY, NOVEMBER 19, 2013

House of Representatives,
Subcommittee on Africa, Global Health,
Global Human Rights, and International Organizations,
Committee on Foreign Affairs,
Washington, DC.

The subcommittee met, pursuant to notice, at 10 o'clock a.m., in room 2172 Rayburn House Office Building, Hon. Christopher H. Smith (chairman of the subcommittee) presiding.

Mr. SMITH. The subcommittee will come to order, and good morning to everyone.

Today's hearing is not being called an emergency hearing, but it could very well be, because since we first decided to hold a hearing to spotlight the human rights situation in the Central African Republic, the situation has deteriorated even further, so that today the country is on the verge of a humanitarian catastrophe.

Coups and dictatorships have characterized the Central African Republic since its independence in 1960, but the current crisis is far more dangerous than what has come before.

Consider this, in a country of approximately 5 million people, roughly 1.1 million citizens face serious food insecurity. Some 460,000 CAR nationals are displaced, including 64,000 who have fled to neighboring countries as refugees and nearly 400,000 who are internally displaced.

This is because there has been a complete breakdown of law and order in the country following the ouster of President Francois Bozize in March of this year. After riding to power on the back of an insurrection known as Seleka, the current dictator, Michel Djotodia, has found it difficult to disengage.

Seleka, originally a political alliance, has transformed itself into a militia of about 25,000 men, up to 90 percent of which come from Chad and Sudan, and, therefore, constitute in the eyes of many, a foreign invasion force. They do not speak the local language and are Muslim in a nation that is roughly 80 percent Christian.

They have targeted churches for destruction and stirred up sectarian hatreds where none had existed previously. Indeed, the Sudanese contingent in particular are said to be members of the notorious Janjaweed, who have spread slavery and destruction into the Darfur region of Sudan and now are doing the same in the Central African Republic.

And if that is not bad enough, elsewhere the Lord's Resistance Army, or the LRA, under the psychotic leader Joseph Kony, is also loose in the Central African Republic. Both the LRA and Seleka are said to kidnap children to serve as soldiers, and UNICEF estimates that there are now as many as 3,500 child soldiers affiliated with armed groups in the country.

Djotodia has formally disbanded Seleka, but Seleka continues to wreak destruction in the countryside, and they have seized mines and other resources in the country. Even in Bangui, the situation is chaotic.

One of our witnesses, Mike Jobbins, has related how ''there have been nearly a dozen successful or attempted carjackings of humanitarian vehicles over the past 2 weeks and at least three aid workers have lost their lives since the crisis began.''

In response the victims have begun to form self-defense units referred to as anti-balaka or anti-machete gangs, which have begun to commit retaliatory outrages of their own. Rather than confront Seleka rebels who are responsible for starting the cycle of violence, they often target Muslim citizens who they deemed soft targets. Thus, the violence begets more violence.

The situation is so bad that just this past week John Ging, the director of the U.N. Office for Coordination of Humanitarian Affairs warned, ''We are very, very concerned that the seeds of a genocide are being sown.'' All of this is happening in a state which, by any definition, is dysfunctional.

In the words of the Prime Minister, who is the closest thing to a legitimate figure in the Government of the Central African Republic, and whom my staff and I met with this summer when he visited Washington, the Central African Republic is ''anarchy, a non-state.'' This descent into chaos has compounded the misery of the people of the Central African Republic, who have suffered greatly and lagged substantially in terms of development. Prior to this year, the Central African Republic ranked 180 of 186 countries per the U.N. Human Development Index.

One area where the Central African Republic did lead bespeaks an irony. National Geographic ranks the Central African Republic as the nation least affected by light pollution. This, of course, is indicative of its low level of development, and the neglect and affirmative harm which generations of political leaders have subjected the country and its people.

Amid this darkness, however, there are some bright spots. It is the leadership of the churches and the faith-based organizations, as well as traditional Muslim leaders, long resident in Central African Republic, who have sought to defuse communal tensions. These indigenous Muslim leaders who speak for peace need to be recognized and distinguished from foreign fighters from countries such as Sudan—the same Janjaweed, again, who harrowed Darfur—who kill and sow destruction in the name of jihad.

We will have the opportunity to hear from one such courageous faith leader, Bishop Nongo. I had the privilege of hosting Bishop Nongo in my office when he came to visit Washington this past summer, and I was moved nearly to tears as he described the suffering of the people of his country. It is leaders such as Bishop Nongo who provide assistance to all, regardless of their affiliation, and who strive for peace, who provide the greatest hope for the Central African Republic.

I would like to now turn to the ranking member and my friend, Ms. Bass.

Ms. BASS. As always, thank you, Mr. Chairman, for your leadership on this issue and today's hearing.

Deputy Assistant Secretary Jackson and today's other witnesses, thank you for coming before this committee and providing testimony, and I would like to officially welcome you. I believe this is your first time giving testimony before our committee.

The crisis in the Central African Republic is deeply concerning, and I hope today's proceedings will offer some clarity on what can be done by the Congress to ensure greater peace and stability in Central Africa and the Central African Republic.

Today we turn our attention to another crisis, this time in the Central African Republic, at the very center of Africa. CAR is the size of Texas with a population equivalent to that of South Carolina. The irony of a country like the Central African Republic is that it is mineral-rich, diamonds, gold, and other deposits. Despite such natural wealth, that wealth does not extend to the people.

CAR has a per capita GDP of $454, a literacy rate of just over 50 percent, and the country's life expectancy stands roughly at 50 years. In comparison, the U.S. had the same rate over 100 years ago in the early part of the 20th century.

The World Food Programme reports that more than ½ million people are currently at risk of hunger. A recent U.N. press release noted that in the CAR 1.6 million people are in dire need of assistance, including food, protection, health care, water, sanitation, and shelter.

In October, before the U.N. Security Council, the Central African Republic's Ambassador to the U.N. referred to his country as a failed state, and the U.N. Envoy to the CAR warned that the country runs the risk of descending into anarchy and chaos. Today's hearing is about a country on the brink of collapse, a fragile state by all accounts. While debate may go on as to the Central African Republic's failed state status, the fact that we are here discussing this situation requires all of us to find better strategies and better solutions.

In early October, I had the opportunity to meet with the Central African Republic's Prime Minister. He was unequivocal in seeking support for his nation. I hope that today's hearing helps clarify the role the U.S. and other nations can play toward saving lives, renewing peace, and returning stability to the Central African Republic.

I want to conclude by saying the African Union is advancing efforts to strengthen peacekeeping efforts. I am eager to hear what role the U.S. sees as these efforts move forward. I am also eager to hear the status of Seleka forces and what can be done to end Muslim Christian violence.

I am keenly aware that the humanitarian crisis has the potential to worsen. If the Republic continues its downward spiral, what impact will all of this have on U.S. counterterrorism efforts, particularly as we deal with the AQIM, the Lord's Resistance Army, and other rogue groups?

Thank you, and I look forward to your testimony.

Mr. SMITH. Thank you very much.

Mr. Cicilline.

Mr. CICILLINE. Thank you, Mr. Chairman, and Ranking Member Bass for holding today's hearing on this very important issue. The relationship between the United States and Africa has been, and continues to be, a priority in U.S. foreign policy. The Central African Republic has had serious obstacles to achieving democracy and stability, and like many of my colleagues I am increasingly concerned about the impact of such instability and insecurity on the region.

Along with strategic considerations, we also must contemplate the humanitarian conditions within the Central African Republic. The United States has a duty to honor the founding principles of our country and to encourage opportunity, prosperity, and the hopes of an upward social mobility. With such rampant food insecurity and internal displacement in the Central African Republic, the workforce cannot truly flourish and citizens will not be able to achieve an adequate standard of living.

There are several questions that must be addressed today regarding the issues that the Central African Republic continues to face, especially its economic and regional stability, and the history of U.S. assistance in addressing these concerns.

I thank Deputy Assistant Secretary Jackson for being here today and look forward to his testimony.

Thank you, Mr. Chairman. I yield back.

Mr. SMITH. Thank you very much.

I would like to now introduce our first distinguished witness, the Ambassador Robert Jackson, who is currently the Principal Deputy Assistant Secretary, Bureau of African Affairs. Ambassador Jackson previously served as our Ambassador to Cameroon and as the Deputy Chief of Mission and Charge d'Affaires at U.S. Embassies in Morocco and Senegal, and has also worked in Burundi, Zimbabwe, Portugal, and Canada.

Within the State Department, he has worked in commercial and consular sections and has done officer training. He also did oversight work in the Office for the Promotion of Democracy and Human Rights after 9/11.

Mr. Ambassador, the floor is yours.

STATEMENT OF THE HONORABLE ROBERT P. JACKSON, PRINCIPAL DEPUTY ASSISTANT SECRETARY, BUREAU OF AFRICAN AFFAIRS, U.S. DEPARTMENT OF STATE

Ambassador JACKSON. Thank you very much, Mr. Chairman, Ranking Member Bass, and Congressman Cicilline. This is an opportunity for the State Department to offer its views on this very important subject.

Seleka, a loose coalition of four rebel groups under the command of the Michel Djotodia, began their violent trek from northeastern Central African Republic (CAR) toward the capital city of Bangui in late 2012. The overthrow of then-President Francois Bozize on March 24 by Seleka forces only exacerbated the crisis. I had been following that crisis from neighboring Cameroon. And after Bozize fled the country, we saw Djotodia declare himself President, suspend the constitution, and dissolve the National Assembly, thus leading the country into greater turmoil.

We are deeply concerned by the extreme levels of lawlessness and violence that continue to plague the country. The United States publicly condemned the Seleka rebellion from the very beginning. Furthermore, the United States Government suspended, as a matter of policy, direct assistance to the Central African Republic central government, but allowed for special funding carveouts that permit NGO-sponsored programs operating in the country focused on humanitarian assistance, civilian protection, health, and antitrafficking in persons activities, all of which focus on vulnerable populations susceptible to violence and instability.

The conflict in the CAR has internally displaced nearly 400,000 people and forced approximately 68,000 new refugees into the Democratic Republic of the Congo, the Republic of the Congo, Cameroon, and Chad. In Fiscal Year 2013, the U.S. Government provided more than $24 million in humanitarian assistance to CAR in support of programs providing food and non-food items, health services, access to clean water, and more.

The State Department also provided $6.2 million to UNHCR and UNICEF to respond to the needs of new refugees in these neighboring countries.

Mr. Chairman, members of the subcommittee, establishing civilian protection in Bangui and the countryside is a prerequisite for a more substantial international presence in assisting the CAR to address the ongoing crisis. In order to help restore peace and assure civilian protection throughout the country, we strongly supported the adoption of U.N. Security Council Resolution 2121, which expressed the Council's support of the African Union-led international support mission in the Central African Republic known as MISCA.

We believe that MISCA is the best mechanism for quickly addressing the ongoing violence in the CAR, facilitating the provision of humanitarian assistance, and establishing the environment necessary for an eventual political transition to take place.

The Department of State now is in the process of notifying the Congress of our intention to provide logistical support, non-lethal equipment, training, and planning assistance to MISCA. We are also urging countries in the region, as well as the broader international community, to assist in facilitating its rapid implementation.

We are concerned that the violence between the largely Muslim Seleka rebels and the self-defense militias that have formed in majority Christian communities in reaction to Seleka's abuses is now taking on an increasingly religious cast. For example, fighting in Bossangoa and Bangassou, between Seleka and local defense militias in September and October sets the stage for what could in a worst-case scenario lead to atrocities on an even larger scale than we have witnessed to date.

On November 8, as part of our continued commitment to working with the international community to find an immediate solution aimed at ending the violence and creating stability in the CAR, the State Department's senior advisor for CAR traveled to Bangui for the first time to participate in the third meeting of the International Contact Group.

This frank and honest discussion resulted in the Bangui Declaration, which calls for the international community to strengthen the AU-led MISCA military mission and to lend support for the CAR's transitional road map. While in Bangui, the United States led the discussion calling on President Djotodia to reverse his plan to enlist former Seleka rebels into the CAR military.

We strongly oppose the trend of past authoritarian leaders in CAR using the military as an instrument of personal power instead of national defense. We have utilized this and other diplomatic engagements, including lengthy discussions with the Government of France in Paris last week, as a means to urge regional and international partners to provide troops, additional funding, and other support necessary for MISCA to deploy quickly into CAR.

We also use these opportunities to press our international partners to join us in looking for ways to bolster the legitimate portions of the transitional government, including Prime Minister Tiangaye, so that governance can begin to be restored to the country and we can begin focusing on holding elections by February 2015, as called for in the political agreements that brought an end to the fighting earlier this year.

We hope, through these engagements, that we will have an increased commitment by the international community to be more engaged on the serious issues facing the CAR.

Chairman Smith, Ranking Member Bass, Congressman, let me assure you that we remain substantively engaged and will continue to address the ongoing crisis in the CAR. There is no doubt that the international community must act quickly. We are committed to working with our international partners to bring about peace and security for the people of the Central African Republic.

We also look forward to keeping you and the committee informed of our efforts in this regard. I would be glad to answer any questions you may have.

[The prepared statement of Mr. Jackson follows:]

Testimony of Principal Deputy Assistant Secretary Robert Jackson

Bureau of African Affairs, U.S. Department of State

House Foreign Affairs Committee

Subcommittee on African Affairs, Global Health, Human Rights and International Organizations

November 19, 2013

Thank you very much Chairman Smith, Ranking Member Bass, and Members of the Subcommittee for the opportunity to testify before you today on this most important subject. We are deeply concerned about the continuing insecurity, humanitarian crisis and human rights violations across the Central African Republic (CAR). We are working closely with our European allies, the United Nations, and the African Union to press for stability, the respect of human rights and the restoration of democratic governance in CAR.

The crisis in the Central African Republic began in December 2012 when Seleka forces, a loose coalition of four rebel groups, under the command of Michel Djotodia, began their violent trek from the northeast region of the country toward the capital city of Bangui, which I had been following from neighboring Cameroon. After rejecting the power-sharing arrangement that had been brokered in January in Libreville, Gabon, by the Economic Community of Central African States (ECCAS), Seleka rebels were able to take the capital Bangui, by force on March 24. President Bozize fled the country, and Djotodia declared himself president, suspended the constitution, and dissolved the national assembly. After significant pressure from the region, Djotodia chose to abide by the ECCAS-brokered arrangement with opposition leaders. This agreement and a second ECCAS summit in April led to a new power-sharing arrangement, the drafting of an interim constitution, and the swearing-in of Djotodia as interim President of the Transition in August. In accord with agreements brokered by ECCAS, Djotodia also promised to hold elections by February 2015.

Djotodia has never had strong command and control of his own Seleka forces and has been unable to sustain them in the field with salaries and stipends. With the collapse of the former national armed forces, the Central African Armed Forces (FACA), and the absence of any other meaningful government authority outside of the capital, relatively autonomous Seleka commanders – including Chadian and Sudanese militia leaders with groups of loyal fighters under them -- have become criminal enterprises preying on local populations. Seleka's targeted violence – including murders, rapes, robberies, looting and burning of villages has created inter-religious tensions in a country that had previously enjoyed excellent Christian-Muslim relations. These Seleka abuses, in turn, have given rise to primarily Christian self-defense groups that have sought to kill both Seleka fighters and CAR Muslims, creating a dangerous dynamic of inter-religious hatred and tension that risks spiraling out of control. For example, fighting in Bossangoa and Bangassou between Seleka and local defense militias in September and October 2013, although primarily an anti-Seleka backlash, has the potential to lead to large-scale atrocities.

The United States, along with others in the international community, have publicly condemned Seleka's overthrow of the government from the very beginning. In early April, as a matter of policy, the United States government decided to suspend direct assistance to the CAR central government, but allowed support for programs operated by non-governmental organizations (NGOs). These programs provide for humanitarian assistance throughout accessible areas in CAR, and combat trafficking in persons, and civilian protection in support of the counter-Lord's Resistance Army campaign.

So far, the conflict in the CAR has internally displaced nearly 400,000 people and forced approximately 68,000 new refugees into the Democratic Republic of the Congo (DRC), the Republic of the Congo, Cameroon, and Chad. This has brought the total number of CAR refugees in neighboring countries to over 220,000. During Seleka's advance on Bangui, hospitals, schools, and warehouses were looted and entire villages destroyed. Today, Internally Displaced Persons (IDPs) have little to no access to clean water, schools, or health services. The ongoing conflict and displacement raises particular concern for the protection of civilian populations. Food security is a growing concern as many farmers missed the planting season due to the violence. U.S. government partners continue to try to reach these populations with life-saving assistance, but are constrained by lawlessness and banditry. In Fiscal Year 2013, the U.S. government provided more than $24 million in humanitarian assistance in CAR to support programs providing food and non-food items, health services, access to clean water, and more. The UN Humanitarian Air Service, supported by USAID and the State Department, continues to provide access to affected populations that are otherwise inaccessible. On September 25, the State Department announced an additional $6.2 million contribution to respond to the needs of new refugees in neighboring countries.

We continue to call on all armed groups in this conflict – primarily the Seleka and an increasing number of self-defense groups -- to refrain from violence, including attacks against innocent women and children. Establishing civilian protection in Bangui and the countryside is a prerequisite to a more substantial international presence in addressing the ongoing humanitarian, human rights, and political crisis. In order to help restore peace and ensure civilian protection throughout the country, we strongly supported the adoption on October 10 of UN Security Council resolution 2121, which expressed the Council's support of the African Union-led International Support Mission in the Central African Republic (MISCA).

We believe MISCA is the best mechanism for quickly addressing the ongoing violence in the CAR. Establishing a secure environment is necessary for the provision of humanitarian assistance and for an eventual political transition to take place. To help MISCA deploy in as rapid and effective a manner as possible, the Department of State has identified and is now in the process of notifying Congress of our intention to provide logistical, non-lethal equipment, training, and planning assistance to MISCA. We are closely coordinating with our international partners who are supporting MISCA. We continue to urge countries in the region, as well as the broader international community, to assist in facilitating the mission's rapid deployment.

While we continue to receive credible reports of human rights abuses against civilians, we know that these reports, alarming as they are, are almost certainly not comprehensive. The lack of access to significant parts of the country is deeply concerning. We continue to receive reports from credible international human rights NGOs that humanitarian workers in the CAR assisting victims of the crisis have been physically harassed, intimidated, beaten, and killed by Seleka rebels. Individuals suspected of committing these crimes are unlikely to face justice while insecurity and instability reign. It is important that all reports of human rights violations be investigated and violators be brought to justice. Therefore, we have supported the UN Security Council decision to reinforce the mandate of the UN Integrated Peacebuilding Office in the Central African Republic (BINUCA) in order to monitor and report on the human rights situation.

We support the Council's decision for BINUCA, as part of its mandate to investigate human rights abuses, to report to the UN Security Council regularly on individuals or groups who are responsible for serious human rights abuses. Furthermore, we also strongly support the UN Human Rights Council's decision in September to establish an Independent Expert to monitor the human rights situation. The State Department along with USAID is examining potential assistance for monitoring, atrocity prevention and/or transitional justice.

Furthermore, we believe the international community must continue to demand that the transitional CAR government end any and all support to the Seleka rebels; exclude rebels responsible for human rights abuses from the reconstituted military, gendarmerie, and police; and abide by the agreements that established the transitional government, including abiding by the electoral timeline of February 2015 and the ban on members of the transitional government contending for office. The United States also co-sponsored a September 2013 resolution with African nations in the UN Human Rights Council (HRC) that called for adherence to the electoral timeline. The Department of State will seek opportunities to express support for this timeline both bilaterally and multilaterally, understanding that security needs to be restored throughout the country and the new constitution needs to be completed in order for elections to be feasible.

We also continue to work to address the crisis in CAR with our regional and international partners through the International Contact Group(ICG) for CAR. On November 8, as part of our continued commitment to working with the international community to find an immediate solution aimed at ending the violence and creating stability in the CAR, the State Department Senior Advisor for CAR traveled to Bangui for the first time to participate in the third meeting of the ICG. The African Union chaired the third Contact Group meeting in Bangui, with more than 40 countries represented, including many regional states and a handful of non-African countries. The Contact Group released the Bangui Declaration, which calls for the international community to strengthen the AU-led MISCA military mission and support the CAR political transition roadmap. It also expresses alarm over the current humanitarian crisis and calls for robust international donor support. During the meeting, Republic of the Congo President Sassou, who has led ECCAS' efforts to respond to the crisis in CAR and restore stability, stated his strong opposition to delaying national elections beyond 2015 and voiced his support that transitional government officials not be allowed to stand for elections.

The United States led the discussion calling for President Djotodia to reverse his plan to integrate 3,500 former Seleka rebels into the CAR security forces and another 1,500 additional Seleka rebels to be recruited as law enforcement officers and park rangers. We emphasized that Djotodia's plan to include large numbers of unvetted and functionally illiterate Seleka fighters was a clear violation of United Nations Security Council Resolution 2121, which calls for a professional, balanced, and representative (by ethnic group, region, and religion) national military force. We strongly oppose the trend of authoritarian leaders in the CAR using the military as an instrument of personal power instead of an instrument of national defense for all citizens.

While in Bangui, the State Department's senior advisor on CAR made it a priority to meet with local and international civil society representatives, in addition to senior government officials. One local NGO, for example, reported that ten women per day came to their Bangui offices from April to August to report being raped; since September, five women per day report being raped. Undoubtedly, the number of rapes since Seleka started its advance is much higher as stigmatization causes the majority of rapes to go unreported. This violence also continues with total impunity since not one accused rapist has yet to be brought to trial.

We have also received reports from local civil society representatives of secret detention centers run in Bangui by the so-called "Extraordinary Committee for the Defense of Democratic Gains." According to our contacts, torture is being carried out at the Roux military camp and another location in Bangui, according to at least 15 victims of torture who have spoken to human rights groups in Bangui.

It was also obvious that fear and tension still pervades the capital as Bangui's streets at night were largely devoid of citizens. Djotodia's announcement in September that he had dissolved the Seleka force was nothing more than a smoke screen as Seleka fighters continue to carry weapons and deny the use of arms to "legitimate" law enforcement authorities whose efforts are needed to end the lawlessness in the CAR.

We are deeply concerned that Djotodia does not intend to abide by his commitment to hold elections by February 2015, but will instead continue to take other measures to delay them and further consolidate his hold on power. His nomination on October 8 of Seleka fighters to take command of 10 of 12 military regions of the country, was a worrying indication of his real intentions. The commitment of Djotodia to even the notion of a unified republic in the CAR is also in doubt. On multiple occasions in recent weeks, Djotodia has told foreign interlocutors that if pushed too hard he might lead the north in seceding from the CAR.

We will continue our diplomatic efforts to coordinate with our partners and to highlight our own commitment to helping address the issues facing the CAR. As our immediate priority, we will continue to work assertively with the French and other members of the international community to bolster efforts to establish security in the CAR. We will continue to utilize these and other engagements, including constructive consultations with the government of France in Paris last week, as a means to urge regional and international partners to provide troops, additional funding, and other support necessary for MISCA to deploy quickly into CAR. We also use these opportunities to press our international partners to join us in looking for ways to bolster responsible stakeholders in the transitional government, including Prime Minister Tiangaye, so that governance can begin to be restored to the country and we can begin focusing on holding elections by February 2015. We hope these engagements will result in increased commitment by the international community to be more engaged on issues facing the CAR.

Finally, let me also note that we remain concerned about the continued activity of the Lord's Resistance Army (LRA) in southeastern CAR. This year, the LRA has continued to commit attacks against civilians across the Mbomou, Haut-Mbomou and Haut-Koto prefectures of the CAR. According to the UN Office for the Coordination of Humanitarian Affairs (UNOCHA), from January to September 2013, presumed LRA fighters committed 21 attacks, resulting in 33 deaths and 128 abductions in the CAR. According to UNOCHA, an estimated 21,000 Central Africans remain internally-displaced and over 6,000 are living as refugees as a result of the LRA threat. The United States continues to support efforts by the regional forces of the AU Regional Task Force (AU-RTF) to end the LRA threat and bring its top commanders to justice. AU-RTF operations have resumed in the CAR, but remain limited by the insecure environment. With the support of U.S. military advisors, we believe the AU-RTF continues to make progress to degrade the LRA's capabilities and promote defections from the LRA's ranks.

Chairman Smith and Members of the Committee, let me assure you that we remain substantively engaged and will continue to address the ongoing crisis in the CAR. There is no doubt that the international community must act quickly. A wide range of U.S. departments and agencies are working to bring to bear all of the appropriate policy tools at our disposal, and we are committed to working with our international partners to bring about peace and security for the people of CAR. We also look forward to keeping you and the Committee informed regarding our efforts in this regard. I would be glad to answer any questions you may have.

—————

Mr. SMITH. Mr. Ambassador, thank you very much for your testimony. And, without objection, your full statement will be made a part of the record. Can you clarify whether U.S. troops are operating inside the Central African Republic as has been reported? Are they helping to support efforts against the Lord's Resistance Army? What is their role?

Ambassador JACKSON. Thank you, Mr. Chairman. Indeed, we do have U.S. troops in the Central African Republic acting as advisors, and their only mission is to combat the Lord's Resistance Army and to support the AU, primarily Ugandan mission, to counter the Lord's Resistance Army and encourage defections and, of course, find Joseph Kony.

Mr. SMITH. You stated in your testimony, orally as well as on page 5 of your written testimony, that the U.S. has led discussions calling for President Djotodia to reverse his plan to integrate 3,500 former Seleka rebels into CAR security forces and another 1,500. What has been the outcome of those interventions? And could you, for the committee, elaborate on the composition of Seleka?

Ambassador JACKSON. Mr. Chairman, allow me to begin with the latter part of your question. We believe that Seleka originally numbered around 4,000 people. It has grown over the months since the rebellion began to about 20,000. While we have no exact count, there is anecdotal evidence to suggest that perhaps three-quarters of that 20,000 originate in Chad or Sudan.

As for the integration of those Seleka forces into the police and the Army, we have made it very clear that we cannot support President Djotodia's efforts to do that. The Bangui Declaration and efforts by our partners in the International Contact Group we hope will lead him to rethink that entire approach.

There is no question that the CAR needs an effective Army and an effective police force, but it needs to be representative of all the people and of all religious groups in the country.

Mr. SMITH. With regards to MISCA, you point out that you believe that MISCA is the best mechanism for quickly addressing the ongoing violence in the CAR. MISCA is, what, about 2,500 troops? How robust are their rules of engagement? One of my biggest takeaways from multiple trips to Africa, and elsewhere, including the former Yugoslavia during the worst days of the bombings and the killings in Sarajevo, was a lack of a mandate to truly be peacemakers rather than to be garrisoned.

I saw the same thing in the DR Congo on trips years ago, and my first trip to Darfur saw the same thing as well—rules of engagement that were far less robust. What are their rules of engagement?

Ambassador JACKSON. Thank you, Mr. Chairman. It is worth nothing that the U.N. mission is actually called a peace-building mission, precisely because we need rules of engagement that are very clear that permit peace to be restored. This is not a peacekeeping mission, unfortunately. We hope eventually it will transition to a peacekeeping mission under AU's auspices.

But the key is that right now the 2,500 troops from the Economic Community of Central African States that are on the ground, plus another 1,500 we expect from those countries as well as Burundi and potentially other AU members, will be able to restore peace, and they are currently engaged in fighting and cleanup operations and any operation necessary to restore peace. So they have robust rules of engagement, and we think appropriate rules of engagement for the situation.

Mr. SMITH. Are there any funding or resource issues, you know, lack of materiel, money, to buy bullets for MISCA, for example, and weapons. Are there deficiencies there?

Ambassador JACKSON. Mr. Chairman, we plan to request the Congress' approval to provide about $40 million for MISCA's operations.

Mr. SMITH. When will that be?

Ambassador JACKSON. Within the next few weeks. We are actively working on using several different pots of money in order to have sufficient funds for this worthy mission. The assistance that we would provide would be non-lethal and would be complemented by assistance from France and the European Union in particular, that would include military supplies to ensure that MISCA can fulfill its peacebuilding mission.

Mr. SMITH. Are there any inhibitions with regards to training that need to be overcome vis-à-vis the Leahy amendment? I mean, I strongly support the Leahy amendment, but as we have recently seen, at least I have seen recently in Nigeria, there are capacities and capabilities that are not being used because the Leahy amendment, out of an abundance of caution, people are less likely to want to train and vet individual soldiers who then could be deployed who have a human rights mindset.

Ambassador JACKSON. Mr. Chairman, I am not aware of any impediments to deploying the soldiers that we plan to train and see in MISCA. That said, we will of course comply with the Leahy vetting requirements to ensure that human rights abusers are not part of the mission. Given the makeup of Seleka and the whole history of this rebellion and the gross human rights violations that have taken place in CAR, adding people with a poor human rights record would only aggravate the situation.

Mr. SMITH. Let me ask you, if I could, on Friday, November 1, United Nations Special Advisor on the Prevention of Genocide, Mr. Adama Dieng, asserted that violence in the country may already constitute crimes against humanity and war crimes. Civilians face imminent threats of atrocities, and he would not rule out the possibility of genocide. Has this risen to the point of genocide?

Ambassador JACKSON. Mr. Chairman, I do not believe we are in a genocidal situation. We are in a pre-genocidal situation, as the U.N. Envoy and other experts have said. And that is why we think it is so important to move ahead with assuring that MISCA is in place next month, so that we can stop the descent into worse and worse violence, and particularly into communal violence.

Mr. SMITH. Is the administration making any plans for a justice mechanism, the likes of which we saw in Sierra Leone, with a tribunal or some way to significantly hold perpetrators of violence to account?

Ambassador JACKSON. We have begun to discuss with the U.N. and partners the possibility of sanctions. We do not currently have enough information to apply sanctions to any individuals. We are in an information-gathering mode at this time, but it is something that is under consideration.

Mr. SMITH. Finally, just let me ask you, as you know, Bishop Nongo is here to provide testimony, among others, in our second panel. The church is playing—and, again, having just been in Jos, Nigeria, different country, but situations that may parallel at least what is going on here, and that's the Boko Haram and its killing spree that they have unleashed, one of the biggest takeaways that I have had time and again and had it most recently with Nigeria was just how effective, how proactive, and how comprehensive the work is that the churches provide, and that they do reach out in a very significant way to the Muslims.

I mean, the highest ranking Islam Muslim cleric in Jos couldn't have been closer to the Catholic Bishop in Jos working together to try to mitigate the violence. And Bishop Nongo will speak shortly about the efforts the church is making to try to provide safe haven shelter, humanitarian assistance, but also to try to bridge the gap between those who commit violence and to put as much of a tourniquet on this terrible blood-letting.

What is your view of the church's role? And how would you characterize the Catholic Church and the other churches' role in CAR?

Ambassador JACKSON. The church and other religious leaders have played a fundamental role in attempting to address this cycle of violence. The Archbishop of Bangui, a prominent Protestant pastor, and one of the leading imams from Bangui, have been working very actively and very effectively together to sensitive their congregants to the dangers of intercommunal violence. And I believe that the Bishop will certainly amplify on that, but we view their role as pivotal and potentially of great relevance in resolving the tensions that have developed over the last year.

Mr. SMITH. And are we backing that up with financial support to them, especially as it relates to the work that they do on behalf of victims? Again, another takeaway, as I met with the Bishop in Jos, I was shocked and disappointed that under PEPFAR he had received money for AIDS orphans, and as we were talking about the Boko Haram and the violence and all the things that he was doing, he said he was bewildered as to why his funding had been shut off for these AIDS orphans.

When I got back to the Embassy, I learned to my shock that only 9 percent of our money, health money and PEPFAR money, was going to faith-based organizations on a continent where faith-based is the go-to entity. And I am wondering if we are assisting tangibly the Bishop and the others, the Protestants, the other faith-based organizations in their humanitarian endeavors.

Ambassador JACKSON. Mr. Chairman, I am going to have to get back to you on that. Of the $25 million that we provided in humanitarian assistance last fiscal year, I do not know how much went to faith-based organizations.

Mr. SMITH. Could you get back specifically with that? And I would hope—and I don't know if it parallels in CAR, but I would hope—I mean, I was disappointed and asked them to try to do a better job certainly in Nigeria, because the story from the Bishop in Jos was frightening. He goes, ''What do I do with these hundreds of children?'' And, again, these are AIDS orphans who all of a sudden he is told, ''Oops, your program has been terminated.'' Please take that back.

Ms. Bass.

Ms. BASS. Thank you, Mr. Chair.

I wanted to know if you could speak a little more about humanitarian assistance that we are providing, to what scale it is specifically, and then also if it is being able to reach the west where the attacks on civilians have been particularly harsh.

Ambassador JACKSON. Congresswoman, I don't have a good sense of the geographical distribution of the assistance. I can tell you that we have provided some assistance in the west and northwest. We are attempting to reach the most affected populations around the country. We have provided food, we have provided access to clean water, we have provided other vital supplies. But to get into the details I would need to get back to you.

Ms. BASS. No problem. And you mentioned that soon you were going to be coming for $40 million for MISCA, and I am assuming that is money that State already had and you wanted redistributed. Are you going to be asking for additional resources for humanitarian efforts as well?

Ambassador JACKSON. We are looking at all of the Central African Republic's needs. At this time, we are focused first and foremost on supplying MISCA with the resources that it needs. We will continue to provide humanitarian assistance from existing programs, and we are looking at how we can support the U.N mission and its efforts to assure that we have the best possible elections by February 2015.

Ms. BASS. Okay. And please follow up with me about the humanitarian assistance, in particular if there are additional resources that are needed, because I would like to be supportive of that.

And I wondered also if you would talk about some of the regional dynamics, because I think you said that three-quarters—well, actually, before getting to that, you talked about the Seleka forces increasing from either 2,000 or 3,000 to 20,000. And so I wanted to know if you would say a little more about that, the reason why their ranks have swelled so much. I am imagining it is for economic reasons that people have joined in, but maybe it is not. Maybe it is ideological or religious.

But I also think you said that three-quarters are from Chad. So, one, why the troops have, you know, swelled; and then, two, the regional dynamics of them being from Chad.

Ambassador JACKSON. We believe that three-quarters of Seleka are from Chad and Sudan.

Ms. BASS. Oh, okay.

Ambassador JACKSON. The two countries. I can't give you a breakdown. I don't think there has been any kind of census. But, indeed, our assessment is that the motivation has been primarily economic. Seleka has consistently pillaged and sent goods that have been pillaged out of the country primarily to Chad and Sudan, and that is part of our basis for concluding that those are the national origins of many of the fighters.

But the rebellion grew in size precisely because people saw economic opportunity, be it illicit in this case, and they profited from it and continue to profit from it. Seleka continues to have access to customs revenues and other revenues that should rightfully be supporting the national government and the people of the Central African Republic.

Ms. BASS. So what does that say, that the majority of folks are not even from the Central African Republic, in terms of the support for Seleka within the country?

Ambassador JACKSON. I am not certain that we can say very much except that these people are mercenaries. There are a lot of questions about how Seleka was financed at its origins, and, unfortunately, we have yet to establish good facts to support various rumors that we have heard.

Ms. BASS. Can you speak to some of the rumors?

Ambassador JACKSON. Some of the rumors are that there were financiers from Chad and Sudan. But, again, those are unfounded.

Ms. BASS. Right.

Ambassador JACKSON. Or unproven, I should say.

Ms. BASS. So then, on a governmental level, perhaps you could talk about the regional powers. I understand the rogue elements, but, you know, are you saying that it is the Government of Chad? What about Uganda, Republic of Congo, et etcetera?

Ambassador JACKSON. The regional countries have actually played a very constructive role. President Deby Itno of Chad has been very active working with President Sassou Nguesso of the Republic of the Congo, in attempting to broker peace deals along the way, starting with the Libreville Accords, and then meeting with the African Union in August, and then President Sassou-Nguesso chaired the most recent contact group meeting in Bangui.

So the regional leaders have been very positive. Gabon, Cameroon, and Equatorial Guinea have also contributed peacekeepers to the overall force. And I must say, the police from the Republic of the Congo have performed exceptionally well according to many reports. And so we appreciate their involvement, and that gives us hope that this force can be effective if it is expanded through MISCA.

Ms. BASS. Do you think we could assist if we appointed a special envoy? Especially, you know, in the question that Chairman Smith asked about if you thought this was genocide or pre-genocide, if we appointed a special envoy, would that be helpful in terms of preventing it from going in that direction toward genocide?

Ambassador JACKSON. Congresswoman, at this time, we do not think it would be helpful. We have a senior advisor, as well as a desk officer, for Central African Republic. That senior advisor is a person who speaks fluent French, who has participated in the contract group meetings, has had access to very senior officials from the government by telephone on a regular basis, is in daily contact with the locally engaged staff who continue to function at our Embassy in Bangui, and we think he is doing a very good job.

So at this juncture, we think the staffing is appropriate for the situation.

Ms. BASS. Thank you very much.

Mr. SMITH. Thank you. Let me just conclude, Mr. Ambassador, with a few final questions, and perhaps Ms. Bass might have another question or two. In his testimony, the Bishop makes I think a very important point in suggesting that the peacekeepers ought to be put under the United Nations auspices and matriculate to a U.N. Chapter VII mandate, and that troops then could be obviously garnered from other states, probably mostly African states. What is your view on that?

You mentioned $40 million. That is a sizable sum. But, again, if they don't have the mandate, if they don't have the kind of rules of engagement that will lead to a disarming of the perpetrators of violence, it could be an ill-fated peacekeeping force.

Ambassador JACKSON. Mr. Chairman, that is a great question and one that we have given a lot of thought to. At this time, we do not support the creation of a U.N. peacekeeping mission, because we think it would take many months to put in place, and we believe that MISCA would provide the immediate security that CAR needs first and foremost.

So we are focusing on the African-led operation. We believe that it can establish the security that we are seeking and put in place the conditions for elections. And the U.N. peacekeeping proposal may be something we want to look at down the road, but at this time we do not think it is a viable option.

Mr. SMITH. With all respect, could it be looked at simultaneously as MISCA is itself being beefed up? I mean, a transition can be done on a parallel tract, and that would bring more players into it in terms of financial resources. I mean, I don't see what the downside would be, especially since we have had a mandate problem. On my first trip to Darfur, I met with a major name, Ajumbo, who told me while he was there, he said, this is after being with him a day and a half, he goes, "I was in Sarajevo during UNPROFOR, and I have the same mandate here. We walk around giving the appearance of protection, but it is a facade." And he was very, very upset about that. And of course the rules of engagement for the Darfurian peacekeeping were significantly ratcheted up over time.

But initially it was awful, and beyond awful because it gave a false sense of protection to the people. And that is exactly what happened with UNPROFOR, particularly with Srebrenica and all of the other atrocities when peacekeepers were deployed and facilitated, perhaps unwittingly, the violence.

And so I am just wondering, you know, what the downside would be of a simultaneous tract to try to get a Chapter VII mandate.

Ambassador JACKSON. Mr. Chairman, I will take that under advisement and confer with my colleagues at the Department. We still believe that right now MISCA is our best option.

Mr. SMITH. One final question. The Bishop also points out that he is organizing care for over 35,000 people. And I would hope— and if you could be in touch with us, you know, either right after this hearing or within a few days, as to how well our resources are supporting through Caritas or Catholic Relief Services, efforts. And that goes for other NGOs as well, but he has specific numbers of people in his compound that are receiving protection, and, you know, they are in great need.

I mean, that is, frankly, the genesis of this hearing, the meeting that we had with the Bishop several months ago, and it has only gotten worse. And so I do hope you will see how we can beef up that humanitarian assistance to these NGOs and to these church-based groups.

Ambassador JACKSON. Mr. Chairman, we will definitely look at that and respond to you as quickly as possible.

Mr. SMITH. I really appreciate that. Thank you so very much, Mr. Ambassador, and I really appreciate it. Look forward to working with you again going forward.

Ambassador JACKSON. Thank you, Mr. Chairman.

Mr. SMITH. Thank you.

I would like to now welcome our second panel to the witness table, beginning with Bishop Nestor Nongo from the Bossangoa Diocese. He has been the Bishop there since 2012. This year, he is also the Vice President of the Central African Catholic Bishops' Conference. He is a member of the Missionaries of Africa Society and was on mission in Nigeria from 1998 to 2004.

He then filled numerous duties in the Diocese of Strasbourg in France, including chaplain to the Africa Missions College, to the Boy Scouts, and to a state hospital. He was also responsible for the Africa Missions Chapel and pastor to the Terrance de Mission Parish from 2004 to 2012.

We will then hear from Mr. Mike Jobbins. Who is a senior program manager for the Africa Region at Search for Common Ground's Washington headquarters. He supports the design, development, and management of SFCG's conflict prevention programs in Africa, and has led the startup of its work in the Central African Republic.

Mr. Jobbins has 10 years' experience working on violent conflicts in Francophone Africa. Most recently, he was based in the DRC and Burundi, working with Search for Common Ground's violence prevention, security, and sector reform, and refugee reintegration programs. Mike previously worked at the Woodrow Wilson International Center for Scholars' Africa Program.

We will then hear from Mr. Philippe Bolopion from Human Rights Watch. He joined Human Rights Watch as U.N. director in August 2010. Prior to that, he spent 5 years working with the French daily Le Monde as the U.N. correspondent. There he covered a wide range of U.N. issues and traveled to such places as Darfur, eastern DRC, Sri Lanka, Gaza, and Haiti.

He has also worked as a journalist covering the United Nations for France 24 and Radio France International. Prior to working in New York, he was based in Pristina where he reported on the end of the Kosovo conflict in 1999 and 2000, so he has a great deal of experience.

Bishop, if you could proceed.

STATEMENT OF THE MOST REVEREND NESTOR-DÉ SIRÉ NONGO-AZIAGBIA, ROMAN CATHOLIC BISHOP OF BOSSANGOA, CENTRAL AFRICAN REPUBLIC

Bishop NONGO-AZIAGBIA. I am Nestor-Desire Nongo-Aziagbia, Bishop from the Diocese of Bossangoa in the Central African Republic, and the Vice President of the Central African Catholic Bishops' Conference.

I want to thank you, Chairman Smith and Ranking Member Bass, for the opportunity to testify today. I ask that my written testimony be entered into the record.

Mr. SMITH. Without objection, so ordered. And I would ask all of you, don't be as concise as sometimes the rules of this and other committees would suggest. We really want to hear what you have to say, so please take whatever time you need.

Bishop NONGO-AZIAGBIA. My diocese and its people are at the epicenter of an unprecedented crisis that began last March. More than 35,000 people have taken shelter in my diocesan compound in horrible conditions to escape the deadly violence. About 440,000 people are displaced in CAR, and no one knows how many people have died.

We believe that about 25,000 people, Seleka and militiamen, are responsible for this violence. Around 90 percent of them have been recruited from Chad and Sudan, and most are Muslims. They do not speak nor understand our local languages.

The victims are overwhelmingly Christian. In response to the attacks, a small but growing number of Christian Central African self-help militia are attacking Muslims. The entire population is living in fear, and the country is now in a state of complete insecurity.

I come to urge you to provide immediate assistance to end the violence. The United States, working with France, the U.N., and the African Union should fund an increase of MISCA troops to secure the entire country the size of Texas, and equip the force to disarm and demobilize the mercenaries and to return them to their home countries and then integrate the Central African citizens back into our society.

This force should be put under a U.N. Chapter VII mandate to ensure impartiality and legitimacy, to use force as a last result, to save innocent civilian lives. We are grateful for the $40 million under discussion by the administration for this purpose.

Second, the United States and its partners should fund humanitarian assistance to allow Central Africans to return to their villages and to rebuild their lives. Catholic Relief Services is working effectively with the church and will be a natural partner in these efforts. We are thankful for the $24 million committed for this purpose. It is a good start, but more is needed.

Third, the United States and its partners should fund the transition process through a legitimate democratically elected government. We need an independent electoral commission to conduct free and fair elections. Assistance should also be extended to civil society and faith-based groups, so they can protect the civil rights and ensure government leaders serve the common good.

At this difficult time, the church is the only national institution that is still operating and serving the needs of the victims of violence and destruction.

In ending, I would like to emphasize two important points about the nature of this conflict. First, the March 2013 overthrow of the government was about gaining access to political power. Seleka attacks on Christian communities have created a growing sectarian conflict in CAR that never before existed. That will make the conflict more intractable.

Second, our rich natural resources are funding the current militias and could attract other armed groups, criminal networks, or even terrorist groups looking for a safe place to operate, new recruits, and a source of financing for their operations. This is a formula for persistent regional instability that must be avoided.

We urge the United States to rally the international community in our time of need. This is clearly a moment when you can be a modern-day good Samaritan to the Central African people who have fallen prey to perpetrators of violence and destruction. We hope and pray that the United States will rise to this call and help us rebuild a new free and democratic Central African Republic.

Thank you for your kind attention. I welcome any questions you might have.

[The prepared statement of Mr. Nongo-Aziagbia follows:]

DIOCESE DE BOSSANGOA
B.P. 1728 BANGUI
République Centrafricaine
Courriel : nestorsma12@gmail.com
Tél : (+236) 70 92 12 04
(+236) 72 53 33 10
(+236) 75 40 01 80
(+236) 77 44 11 39

WRITTEN TESTIMONY
BY MOST REVEREND NESTOR-DESIRE NONGO AZIAGBIA

HEARING ON THE CRISIS IN THE CENTRAL AFRICAN REPUBLIC
Submitted to the
HOUSE SUBCOMMITTEE ON AFRICA, GLOBAL HEALTH, GLOBAL
HUMAN RIGHTS AND INTERNATIONAL ORGANIZATIONS

NOVEMBER 19, 2013

I am Most Reverend Nestor-Désiré NONGO AZIAGBIA, bishop from the Diocese of Bossangoa, in the Central African Republic (CAR) and Vice President of the Central African Catholic Bishops' Conference. I want to thank you, Chairman Smith and, Ranking Member Bass, for the opportunity to testify before your Subcommittee. I ask that this written testimony be entered into the record.

I am a religious leader and a pastor to my diocese of about 623,000 people, 360,000 of whom are Catholic. Since early 2013, my diocese and its people have been at the epicenter of an unprecedented crisis. As I speak, more than 35,000 people have taken shelter in my diocesan compound living in horrible conditions to escape the deadly violence occurring just outside our walls. Zenit, a Catholic news service reports that about 2,000 homes have been destroyed in my diocese alone. Some estimate that about 440,000 people are displaced across the country, and no one knows how many people have died. The road south to the capital Bangui, over 200 miles away is deserted. Villagers have fled to escape the attacks, mass killings, rape, and plundering perpetrated by the roaming groups of Seleka militia. Fighting, the mass displacement and economic collapse have disrupted the agricultural planting and harvesting season. The World Food Program estimates that over 1 million people, almost one out of four Central Africans, face serious food insecurity. Seleka groups have also taken control over gold and diamond mines, the primary source of foreign exchange revenue.

The Central African Republic (CAR) is a country of 4.5 million people in the center of the African Continent. In March, CAR experienced a coup d'état led by Michel Djotodia. For its entire 63 year post-colonial history, CAR has been ruled by a series of military coup leaders and negligent autocratic politicians who have plundered the country of its rich natural resources and neglected the needs of their people. As a result, CAR ranks near the bottom of United Nations Human Development Index (180 out of 186 countries). Life expectancy is 49 years. Adults have a mean average of only 3.5 years of education.

This current political crisis is, however, very different and more threatening to the country, its people and the surrounding region than past political upheavals. Before taking power, the current Interim President Djotodia led an alliance of four political parties, called Seleka (Alliance in the Sango language). For years Seleka opposed the rule of former President Francois Bozize. As a result of years of poor governance, corruption, a failed election, political deadlock and a series of broken peace deals, Seleka strengthened its rebel group forces from about 5,000 rebels to 25,000 when Michel Djotodia recruited large numbers of mercenary forces from Darfur, Sudan and southern Chad and took control of the country. At present, we believe the Chadian and Sudanese forces in Seleka make up 90% of the Seleka militia. These foreign mercenaries, who put President Djotodia in power, now run rampant across the country, attacking villages, stealing property and livestock, raping, abducting and killing many people and recruiting child soldiers. Although President Djotodia has formally dissolved Seleka in an attempt to end the violence, he has no formal army to enforce peace and security.

The four main groups of the Seleka militia have established control over different regions of CAR, setting up a *de facto* foreign occupation. Most of the Seleka forces do not speak the local language, come from different ethnic backgrounds, and are Muslim. They occupy a country that is 85% Christian and 12% Muslim. Traditionally, Christians and Muslims in CAR have enjoyed good relations. Seleka's violent attacks have targeted Christian homes, schools and places of worship while sparing local Muslim communities and mosques, often only a short distance away. Christian communities have now begun to set up self-defense militia to fight back. Sadly, there are reports that they are attacking Muslim communities in retribution. Thus, although the violent conflict started out as a response to poor governance and exclusion, and a battle over access to political and economic power, it has now taken on an additional and dangerous Muslim-Christian sectarian character that the country has never experienced.

The Central African Muslim and Christian communities are being divided by another particular aspect of this conflict. Seleka militia often raid villages to steal cattle, livestock and other property. Seleka militia men then pass the livestock to Central African Muslim herders to take care of because like them, herding is part of their shared culture. Inevitably, Christians see local Muslims herding the cattle that Seleka stole from them. This has led some Christians to believe the Central African Muslim community is in league with the Chadian and Sudanese mercenaries and is benefiting from Christian losses. This conflict and the grievances it is creating could create internal Muslim-Christian conflict that will persist even if the foreign mercenaries eventually return to their countries of origin.

Another important factor in this conflict is the presence of gold and diamonds in CAR. Seleka militia groups are already in control of gold and diamond mining areas. There are regular reports of attacks on mining communities in order to take control over mining operations. The potential revenue from this illegal mining will strengthen Seleka forces embed them more firmly in the country and create in CAR a 'conflict minerals' crisis similar to the situation in eastern Democratic Republic of the Congo.

The total absence of the rule of law and the presence of vast natural resource wealth could attract other outside militia groups, criminal networks, or even terrorist groups looking for a safe place to operate, new recruits and a source of financing for their operations. This is a formula for persistent regional instability by fueling militia activities in neighboring countries. This must be avoided at all cost.

For years before the coup d'état in March 2013, northern and northwest CAR have been havens for Chadian rebels and armed groups from Darfur in Sudan. In the last few years, the infamous Lord's Resistance Army has taken refuge in the Southeast of the country to find refuge from Ugandan army forces supported by American troops. They have also pillaged villages, killed innocent civilians and forcefully abducted children into their ranks.

In this situation of chaos, the Catholic Church stands as virtually the only national institution that still functions. In my diocese alone we run 54 schools and seven social welfare centers. I and my staff are organizing care for over 35,000 people. Archbishop Dieudonné NZAPALAINGA of Bangui, the capital of CAR, has united with the President of the Central African Islamic Community and the President of the Evangelical Churches in a religious platform to call on the President and Seleka leaders to end the violence. They are also urging national Muslim and Christian leaders, and their communities, to refrain from violence and counter attacks.

The Church Caritas institutions have mobilized assistance from international organizations like Caritas Internationalis and Catholic Relief Services to feed the displaced. We are also helping people to restart their farms by providing seeds and tools. Lastly, the diocese of Bangassou in the LRA area and CRS are helping villages to develop safety and security plans to provide early warning of LRA movements and help people avoid attacks.

In September I traveled to New York with a delegation of Central African civil society leaders to meet UN officials and country missions to the UN to raise awareness of the crisis and to plead for assistance. I and the delegation also came to Washington where the National Endowment for Democracy, the U.S. Conference of Catholic Bishops and CRS staff organized meetings with Congressional leaders, the U.S. Commission on International Religious Freedom and the State Department.

In October, Archbishop NZAPALAINGA from the Archdiocese of Bangui traveled to Geneva to address the United Nations Human Rights Council to raise awareness of the crisis and to stimulate a mobilization of donor countries to help us bring peace to our country.

I have returned to the United States now to urge you, the United States Government to provide immediate assistance. First, the CAR urgently needs international support to end the violence. The United States working with France, the UN and the African Union should fund an increase of MISCA troops to secure the entire country (the size of Texas) and equip the force to compel Seleka forces to disarm, demobilize and reintegrate into society, or to return to their home countries. This force should be put under a UN Chapter VII mandate to ensure impartiality and the ability to stop violence and save innocent civilian lives.

The UN mandate and operational control is important for two reasons. First it is the need to prevent regional country forces in MISCA from pursuing their national interests over the interests of the CAR people. A large portion of the MISCA troops are from Chad. Chadian government troops protected former President Bozize while he was in power. The Chadian's withdrawal permitted Seleka forces to take control over the entire country. In addition, the largest portion of the Seleka forces are also Chadian.

It is our hope that the UN will be able to select MISCA troops from neutral African countries outside of our immediate region and also monitor all troops' operations to ensure impartiality. The second reason for a UN mandate is the hope that the UN will instill greater discipline and effectiveness.

My second request is that the United States and its partners should fund humanitarian assistance such as food, household goods, health care and agricultural inputs to allow Central Africans to return to their villages and rebuild their lives. A second phase of assistance would help people to rebuild their homes, promote societal reconciliation programs and help the government to re-establish essential social services like schools and health clinics. The Church has a close and effective partnership with Catholic Relief Services on the ground and we urge you to fund projects that take full advantage of the benefits of this productive partnership.

Third, the United States and its partners should fund the transition process to a legitimate, democratically elected government. We need an independent electoral commission to prepare the electoral voter rolls, establish the polling stations and then organize effective monitoring programs to ensure that the electoral campaign, the election day process and the vote counting are done in a free and fair way.

We will need many years of sustained assistance to rebuild government administrative, judicial and social services and professional, well-trained military and police forces under the full authority of civilian leaders. We request the International Criminal Court to investigate the most serious cases of human rights abuses.

We urge you in a particular way to extend ample assistance to civil society and faith-based groups so they can protect the peoples' civil rights and ensure government leaders serve the common good. At this difficult time, the Church is the only national institution that is still operating and serving the needs of the victims of violence and destruction. It is also the only institution big and trusted enough to unite religious leaders to speak truth to the interim government and hopefully be a positive influence on its policies and actions.

In closing, we urge the United States to rally the international community in our moment of need. This is clearly a moment when you can be a modern day Good Samaritan to the Central African people who have fallen prey to perpetrators of violence and destruction. Central Africans look up to the United States as the leader of the community of nations. You are a country and a people who many years ago fought to establish your freedom from a foreign power. You endured a brutal civil war and reunited as one nation to rise to the world power that you are.

We hope and pray that the United States will rise to this call and help us rebuild a new, free and democratic Central African Republic.

Most Reverend Nestor Désiré NONGO AZIAGBIA
Bishop of Bossangoa and
Vice President of the Central African Catholic Bishops' Conference

Mr. SMITH. Thank you so very much, Bishop Nongo.

Mr. Jobbins.

STATEMENT OF MR. MIKE JOBBINS, SENIOR PROGRAMME MANAGER, AFRICA, SEARCH FOR COMMON GROUND

Mr. JOBBINS. Thank you, Chairman Smith, Ranking Member Bass, and members of the committee. I would like to also start by thanking Bishop Nongo for the fantastic work that his diocese is doing in Bossangoa, as well as for Mr. Bolopion for the work that Human Rights Watch is doing in documenting the deteriorating situation in the Central African Republic.

I also ask that my written testimony be entered into the record.

I work for Search for Common Ground, which is one of the largest conflict transformation organizations in the world, and we have been working in Central African Republic since the end of last year, working with Catholic Relief Services to prevent violence using media, using community actions in the southeast, and increasingly around the rest of the country as we see the crisis that we have all noted begin coming out of control.

My testimony is informed by our work on the ground, but the opinions and the analysis are my own.

I would like to share with you three things that we consider critical to understanding the situation in CAR today. The first is looking at the dynamics of the violence, and the second is looking at the trend lines, and the third considering why we think this is a critical time and opportunity to realistically change the course of action and change the course of the tragic river that we are seeing.

The first is on the dynamics of violence. The crimes that have been committed by the Seleka forces are well-documented. Human Rights Watch, Amnesty International, and a great number of very courageous Central African media groups, Central African civil society groups, have documented these amply.

They have documented rapes, killings, arbitrary executions, reprisals against the previous regime, and hundreds and most likely thousands of deaths through those atrocities, both in March and then more recently as we see an uptick in fighting with anti-balaka groups that you mentioned in your opening statement.

The important thing that we are seeing with Seleka is that even though they disbanded in September, they still retain de facto control over much of the country. And, in that regard, the command and control structures have broken down and they are much harder to control and to engage with than in the past.

It is a group without any clear ideology, any clear platform, or anything that unites them except a sense of opportunism, a sense of marginalization, and a shared faith. Many of them are of the Muslim faith.

The second part of the violence that we see is that there has been a breakdown of law and order that has created a vacuum. So the LRA, of course, continues to operate. It has been facilitated because many of the operations were suspended during the uncertainty of the transition period, and then we also see poachers coming down from Sudan, and we see a number of upticks in armed bandits. We have all sorts, and not just Seleka, but new forms of banditry and lawlessness.

And, third, that was alluded to by Bishop Nongo and is certainly troubling is the rising uptick in intercommunity violence. The anti-balaka militias are springing up around the country, and we have seen segregation of nearly every community. Every village, every city, has been dividing into ethnic neighborhoods, into religiously divided neighborhoods.

As a result, with this armament process, with this segregation, with this fear, we see a tinder box in the local political dynamics where any incident can create a spillover. And so not only have we seen violence in the northwest, which has always been a hot bed of opposition to the Seleka movement, but we have also seen incidents in Obo, incidents in Zemio, where farmer and pastoralist tensions have boiled over into intercommunal violence.

The trend lines in all of this are scary. The ingredients for tragedy at a much larger level are there. We saw for the first time in mid-October heavy weapons used by both anti-balaka and Seleka forces, including mortars and ground-to-ground missiles. We see increasing armament around the country and increasing segregation, as well as an economy that is devastated, a population that is desperate, and a political transition that doesn't seem to be advancing very clearly.

This is the same sorts of things that we have seen create frustration and create tragedies in Syria, in the DRC, and elsewhere, and we see those same dynamics at play of segregation, fear, and weaponry.

But yet the situation isn't hopeless. We have heard a lot about the upcoming deployment of MISCA, which is certainly a promising—could be a very promising development if there is sufficient U.S. logistical, financial, and planning support. At the same time, we are also hoping to see security before MISCA gets deployed to secure humanitarian access in the corridors of Bangui.

You alluded to a comment I made in my statement that there have been dozens of attacks on humanitarian vehicles. Those are continuing to increase. And as we lose humanitarian space, it not only affects us but it also affects the entire community that are being served by the humanitarian access.

On the second point on humanitarian response, it is important to underline the operational capacities there—Catholic Relief Services, Mercy Corps, IRC, IMC. Many of the major humanitarian actors are there and have the operational capacity to respond, yet funding is short. The U.N.'s combined appeal only garnered 42 percent of the amount that they requested, and there is a need to ramp up assistance as well as the capacity to do so. There is not yet the funding, as far as we know.

The third point on how to accomplish this process, as you referenced earlier, is a good one and that is the role that the religious community and community-based groups can play. There is a risk that before any peacekeepers come the situation will be already out of control, be too far past the pale, yet there are community leaders who are there now, there are church leaders, there is media, there are youth groups, there are thousands, hundreds of thousands of Central Africans who are deeply upset with what they see going on.

And groups like the church and others can mobilize a response to that in a way that can happen before the peacekeepers and prevent some of these dynamics of segregation and violence from coming to fruition.

And, finally, certainly the transition process is a critical one. We heard from the colleagues from the State Department about the accompaniment of that process, and that is something that we would like to see continue, particularly with a higher level of engagement from the United States, more consistent political engagement.

Certainly, the nomination or the naming of a special advisor is helpful, but at the same time making sure that there is an Embassy that reopens in Bangui as soon as it is feasible from a safety perspective, in the meantime maintaining contact with the transitional authorities, with the civil society, is critical, as these decisions are being sorted out, because without a clear political future, without understanding what is going to happen to the Seleka forces, if there is going to be demobilization, what will happen with the electoral process, it is very unclear what the future of the political leadership is in the country and impossible to find an exit to the crisis in that context.

So those are the four points that we consider priority actions for U.S. engagement, and I am open to your questions. And thank you again for your time.

[The prepared statement of Mr. Jobbins follows:]

Written Testimony

by Mike Jobbins

Submitted to the

House Subcommittee on Africa, Global Health, Global Human Rights, and International Organizations

NOVEMBER 19TH 2013

Members of Congress, Ladies and Gentlemen:

Chairman Smith, Representative Bass, and Members of the Committee, I would like to begin by thanking you for convening this timely and important meeting, and for the chance to update you on the increasingly worrying crisis in the Central African Republic.

I would also like to recognize the extraordinary work that my co-panelists, the distinguished Reverend Nongo-Aziagbia and Mr. Bolopion, and their organizations are doing to raise awareness of the severity of the crisis, and respond to the urgent needs within the CAR.

My name is Mike Jobbins, I work on violence prevention with Search for Common Ground. My testimony is informed by our on-the-ground programs in the Central African Republic, but the views expressed are my own.

I will begin by speaking briefly on the current state of the crisis in the CAR, some of the risks of a further deterioration of conditions there, and then conclude by considering some practical steps to help improve the situation.

THE CURRENT STATE OF CRISIS IN THE CENTRAL AFRICAN REPUBLIC

The politico-military crisis, which the Central African Republic has experienced since late 2012, has taken a new turn. Fighting between the former regime and the *Seleka* rebellion profoundly weakened an already-fragile state.

Prior to the crisis, the Central African Republic ranked 180th out of 187 countries in the world on the UN's Human Development index. The central government had little control outside of Bangui, and was led by an increasingly-narrow group of political elites, including the wife and children of then-President Francois Bozizé, who had himself come to power in a coup in 2003.

A series of long-running rebel movements operated in the north of the country prior to the recent coup, and with porous borders, the Central African Republic became home to foreign armed groups, including the Chadian rebel leader Baba Ladé, the Lord's Resistance Army, and heavily armed Sudanese poachers.

Seleka's arrival in Bangui in March 2013 ushered in a new era of insecurity and chaos. UN Secretary General Ban Ki Moon observed in May that "the country is plunging into a state of general anarchy marked by a complete breakdown of law and order," an observation that has sadly continued to play out over the past eight months. The instability displaced more than 400,000 people, claimed countless lives, and risks to deteriorate further. In the present context, we can see three forms of violence against civilians.

THREE PATTERNS OF VIOLENCE

1. Abuses by semi-organized armed groups, notably the (ex) *Seleka* forces. The *Seleka* movement, officially disbanded since September, still retains *de facto* control in much of the country. Abuses committed by *Seleka* fighters have been well documented by Human Rights Watch, Amnesty International, and national human rights groups, and include arbitrary killings, looting, pillaging, and rape on a large scale.

There had always been little internal cohesion within the *Seleka* movement. *Seleka* came into being as a coalition of fighters from long-running and historically-opposed rebel groups and remained fractious, with troops loyal to individual commanders with only a loose hierarchy. There is no coherent agenda, ideology, or political platform behind the *Seleka* movement, aside from – at most – a general sense that the north of the country has been historically neglected. Apart from being predominantly Muslim, and being driven by opportunism, there is little else that fighters within the *Seleka* movement have in common with one another.

Over the course of the rebellion, the numbers of *Seleka* fighters dramatically increased as its success attracted recruits. It is widely cited that the movement began with 5 000 fighters at the end of 2012 and are now thought to number more than 20 000. While it is impossible to know the exact proportions, local media, civil society, and human rights groups have observed that a large proportion of *Seleka* commanders and fighters come from Chad and Sudan. There are also credible reports of the recruitment of children into the movement, and UNICEF currently estimates that there are now as many as 3 500 child soldiers affiliated with armed groups in the CAR.

The rapid increase in poorly-disciplined fighters, the lack of coherent objectives or community support, and the absence of a clear command-and-control structure, particularly since being officially disbanded, has meant that the majority of *ex-Seleka* fighters have drifted into looting, pillaging, and attempting to continue to reap the spoils of war. This is dangerous for two reasons.

First, the lack of internal control makes it difficult for political leadership to reign in the remnants of the movement. In recent days there have been reports of violence between different groups of Seleka fighters, creating the risk of new waves of violence.

Second, the lack of support structures has led some groups of ex-*Seleka* to try to rally local Muslim civilians to their "cause," and to try to position themselves as protectors of the interests of the Muslim community in places like Yaloké and Bangassou where ex-*Seleka* sought to make common cause with local Muslims when they felt under threat, or in apparent alliances with Peulh herdsmen that cross the region. It is possible that as *Seleka* forces divide and come under threat, this trend of increasingly seeking alliances based on identity-lines at the local level may increase. There are persistent rumors – though no confirmation – of attempts by *Seleka* groups to form alliances with groups from North Africa and the Middle East.

2. Banditry, criminality, score settling, and other opportunistic activity. Alongside the banditry and abuses committed by *ex-Seleka* elements, the breakdown of law and order created an opportunity for other forms of violence. This includes carjackings, highway robberies, and other kinds of criminality, which has further exacerbated insecurity for ordinary citizens. The turmoil that has persisted in the CAR since last December has created a vacuum, in which other criminal groups have operated. This includes the Lord's Resistance Army (LRA), which has operated in the southeastern CAR for years. The Ugandan Army's operations against the LRA were impeded during the crisis, although they have since resumed. In addition to the LRA, in recent days we have seen several movements of heavily armed wildlife poachers moving southwards from Sudan.

3. Inter-communal violence. As a result of the lawlessness and fears of inter-communal strife, many cities, including Bangui, have become increasingly segregated along ethnic and religious lines as people settle in neighborhoods shared with their family members and identity group in order to better ensure their security. Self-defense militias, known as *anti-Balaka*, have emerged in many parts of the country and clashed with ex-*Seleka* elements.

These groups have actively attacked ex-*Seleka* fighters, and in many cases have also explicitly targeted Muslim communities perceived be allies of ex-*Seleka* forces. The targeting of innocent civilians and the practice of "collective punishment" has created the dynamic of attacks and reprisals between communities. The documentation of atrocities committed against civilians, which began primarily in the northwest has increased tensions throughout the country.

The presence of local defense groups to protect a neighborhood or village has existed to various degrees in the past, but we have seen a dramatic proliferation of such groups the country in recent months. Attacks by *anti-Balaka* groups have often triggered "collective punishment" reprisals by ex-*Seleka* forces, particularly targeting young men based on their perceived ethnicity or neighborhood. *Anti-Balaka* groups at the moment do not appear to be organized beyond their immediate surroundings, although a few have proclaimed loyalty and to, and identified with, the former regime.

In addition, while many such groups have been armed with traditional weapons, including hunting rifles and machetes, there have been a few cases of more heavy weapons being used, including a clash at Gbombolo in mid-October that saw artillery use and which left six dead. Later that month, a weapons cache believed to belong to *anti-Balaka* groups was discovered in Bangui including mortar shells, ground-to-ground missiles and Kalashnikov ammunition.

As word of violence spreads throughout the country, it has the result of further increasing tensions, fears, and rumors, creating the risk of a self-perpetuating cycle. For example, in the far southeast prefecture of Haut Mbomou, which has seen relatively little presence of *Seleka* forces, information about attacks elsewhere in the country have led both Muslim and Christian communities to segregate, arm themselves, and view each other with suspicion. As a result, long-running conflicts between predominantly Muslim herders and predominantly Christian farmers have boiled over into serious violence in several places. In the climate of fear, mistrust, and armament, any small incident risks quickly escalating.

This amalgamation of factors places civilians at imminent risk of atrocity crimes. On Friday November 1, United Nations Special Adviser on the Prevention of Genocide, Mr. Adama Dieng, asserted that violence in the country may already constitute crimes against humanity and war crimes, civilians face imminent threat of atrocities, and he would not rule out the possibility of genocide. On November 13th, John Ging, director of the UN Office for Coordination of Humanitarian Affairs warned, "We are very, very concerned that the seeds of a genocide are being sown."

HUMANITARIAN CONSEQUENCES

The humanitarian consequences have been devastating. The United Nations estimates that half of 4.6 million Central Africans are in need of urgent assistance. Nearly 400,000 people have fled their homes, many living in the bush and forests out of fear of being attacked in their villages. The current period, from September to November is harvesting season in much of the country, but people are unable to harvest out of fear of attack. As a result, about 1.1 million people are facing food shortages. The school year should have started last month, but seven out of ten children were unable to return. There are critical shortages in nearly every sector: food, health, shelter, water and sanitation, and education.

Insecurity in Bangui has led to increased pressure on aid workers. There have been nearly a dozen successful or attempted carjackings of humanitarian vehicles over the past two weeks and at least three aid workers have lost their lives since the crisis began. The situation is troubling, and appears to be degrading. Yet, there is substantial humanitarian capacity in the CAR to respond to the crisis. There are about 28 international NGOs operating in the country, including Catholic Relief Services, Mercy Corps, IMC, MSF, IRC and others, as well as UN Agencies like UNICEF and WFP, and the ICRC. While these groups are largely able to secure operational access to provide assistance, there are chronic funding shortfalls and only 42% of the UN's Consolidated Appeal has been met.

THE RISK OF FURTHER DETERIORATION

The humanitarian crisis in the Central African Republic, and its human cost, is troubling. Even more troubling is recognition that we are seeing the ingredients necessary for an even greater tragedy. We see many of the same features emerging in this situation that we have seen in the DRC, Syria, Nigeria and other regions that have seen protracted violence on a large scale. These include:

1. The emergence of a multiplicity of militias closely aligned with ethnic and religious identity groups. As both *Anti-Balaka* and *ex-Seleka* groups seek to rally support, there is a risk of further polarization along ethnic and religious lines;
2. The proliferation of weapons in the country, including from looted government arsenals, but likely also through the international weapons trade. This is accompanied by illicit trafficking in diamonds, cattle, poaching and other transnational criminal activities that have long-existed in the CAR;
3. Increasing popular perception of a sectarian divide, driven by recent experiences of violence;

4. The breakdown of economic and social life, which has exacerbated suffering for ordinary citizens, and driven a sense of frustration and desperation in both rural and urban areas;
5. An unclear political transition process, and an uncertain "endgame" for the transitional leadership and ex-Seleka fighters, should the transition succeed.

RESPONDING TO THE CURRENT CRISIS

There is a manifest need – and a critical opportunity – for the international community, national and international civil society, and local actors to take urgent action to prevent violence, provide lifesaving assistance, and support a path towards a stable transition to civilian rule. While the current situation is troubling, it is not hopeless.

There are promising local initiatives to resolve tensions within the CAR, including a series of interfaith meetings and several examples of ex-*Seleka* commanders being transferred or moved as a result of abuses. Humanitarian organizations on the ground have the capacity to respond, and discussions on a MISCA peacekeeping force appear to be slowly advancing.

There is a realistic chance for a coordinated, strategic, and urgent response by the international community – including the United States – to begin stabilizing the country before the situation deteriorates further. The current moment in CAR represents a key opportunity to head off the worst case scenario, along the principle that "a stitch in time saves nine." To identify what this might look like, we, Search for Common Ground, convened a group of civil society and religious leaders in Bangui in October, and consulted an array of international and local actors on how best to respond to the crisis. We identify four immediate needs:

1. Improving Security. The multiplicity of militia groups, particularly *Seleka* elements have overwhelmed the capacity of FOMAC peacekeepers and the remains of the former armed forces and the Gendarmerie. There is therefore an urgent need for the deployment of the much-anticipated MISCA peacekeeping mission which is sufficiently resourced, with the adequate numbers of troops and mobility, and with a suitable mandate to protect civilians. U.S. logistical, financial and planning support to this mission will be critical to ensure its success. At the same time, there is urgent need for a limited interim force aimed at securing the rapidly-closing humanitarian space and securing the major arteries in Bangui, in order to facilitate the circulation of goods, people, and humanitarian materiel.

Additionally, there is a need for continued strong international engagement to protect civilians, documenting, denouncing and dissuading abuses committed by the different armed groups. This is a role that can be played by a reinforced BINUCA office if rapidly deployed and resourced, under the existing Security Council Resolution. The US can be support these efforts through high-visibility public statements recognizing the gravity of the situation, through its interactions with the Transitional Government, and through its engagement with regional and international partners.

2. Community-Based Violence Prevention. While the rapid deployment of peacekeeping forces are a priority, the current situation risks seriously deteriorating before MISCAs deployment. Even if the challenges posed by armed groups are addressed, the proliferation of weapons and mistrust within communities will create long-running issues if they are not dealt with. There is a need and opportunity for the US to support existing initiatives by civil society, media, the religious community and other local actors to stem the tide of fear and polarization.

We have seen media, civil society and religious leaders successfully mobilize their communities to de-escalate tensions and reject violence in many areas during the height of the 2009-2010 war in Cote d'Ivoire and even in some parts of the Democratic Republic of Congo. The rise of fear and mistrust is not irreversible; the capacity and the potential to change course is present in the Central African Republic as well.

3. Humanitarian response. There is tremendous humanitarian need. Reliable information is difficult, but it is believed that more than half of the entire population requires urgent assistance and nearly every kind of emergency assistance, including health, protection, and food security is necessary. As I noted before, the human and operational capacity exists in country to begin meeting these needs, but there are significant funding shortfalls in order to respond.

4. Transition Planning. Finally, key questions contentious questions remain unresolved, including elections and the political future of the transitional leadership, the potential demobilization of *Seleka* combatants, reconciliation, economic recovery, restoration of the state, and potential transitional justice mechanisms. While these are significant issues requiring long-term sustained effort, they are also intrinsically linked to the interests of actors perpetrating the current wave of violence.

Many of these issues were agreed in the Libreville and Ndjamena political roadmap, but will require significant political accompaniment to put into practice. The U.S. could support this by re-establishing a diplomatic presence in Bangui as soon as feasible or through the option of temporary accreditation in a neighboring country, and increasing contacts with the transitional authorities at all levels, as well as with civil society and other groups.

This is a critical moment for the U.S. government to engage proactively and decisively to protect civilians and prevent current threats from evolving into large-scale atrocities in the Central African Republic. While there are indeed a multitude and complexity of challenges facing the U.S. today, failing to act in CAR today will make it harder and more costly in both lives and dollars for the United States to act tomorrow.

Mr. SMITH. Thank you very much for your time, for your wonderful work on the ground, and for these very specific recommendations. Thank you so much.

I would like to now recognize Mr. Bolopion.

STATEMENT OF MR. PHILIPPE BOLOPION, UNITED NATIONS DIRECTOR, HUMAN RIGHTS WATCH

Mr. BOLOPION. Thank you very much, Mr. Chairman. Thank you very much, Ranking Member Bass. And I would ask that my statement be entered for the record as well.

I work for Human Rights Watch, which is a human rights organization. Three weeks ago I arrived in Bangui. I was carrying piles of our latest report there. It is a brutal read. It is a report that details abuses committed by the Seleka fighters between March and June of this year. For many months now, they have killed scores of civilians, women, children. They have pillaged, burned entire villages, looted as well, and they did this with complete impunity.

So arriving in Bangui, I knew that the situation was very bad, and yet I was not fully prepared for what I found on the ground there. We quickly made our way to Bossangoa, where the Bishop is from, which is in the northern part of the country. And as soon as we arrived there, we saw the Seleka. They are in control; they rule the town. And we saw what they looked like. To be very clear, it is a bunch of very young men wearing random uniforms, flipflops, carrying old weapons, but they are the law in town.

We went to the church, which has now become the center of a makeshift displaced people camp. I have seen my share of camps in my career. I can tell you this is one of the most horrible I have seen. It stinks of human waste. There is smoke everywhere, sick people, children. It is a very, very bad camp.

And the real tragedy is that many of the people I met in this camp live just nearby, some only a few hundred yards from the church. They were not displaced by a natural catastrophe; they were just displaced by fear, because whenever they tried to leave the camp and work in their fields, for example, they get shot at by the Seleka fighters who control the town.

As a matter of fact, in front of the church, I met a young woman roughly my age, Florence Namngafo. She was carrying an infant child there who had a really nasty wound on his arm and he was injured by the same Seleka bullet that killed his father close to their field and for absolutely no reason. And this woman only survived because she played dead for several hours while her kid was screaming in pain, unable to assist him.

Now, if you walk a bit away from the church in Bossangoa, you quickly meet the Muslim communities. You have about 4,000 people. They live around what used to be the school, what used to be the court building, in very poor conditions as well. And these people were not displaced by the Seleka; they were displaced by anti-balaka violence. And, as you have heard, the anti-balaka are these militias of mostly Christians.

They are supposed to be about self-defense, but the story we were told by Muslim residents there are very different. It appears that in many instances these anti-balaka use the same brutal tactics as the Seleka and target civilian Muslims for the only reason that they are Muslims.

So, for example, I talked to a few men there who told me that their village was attacked only months ago by anti-balaka. At 5 o'clock a.m. in the morning, they come in the village where you have also a few Christian people. They go to all the Muslim houses, take everybody out, and started saying things like, ''You are Muslims. You are Seleka. We are going to kill you. We are going to kill all the Muslims.''

They proceeded to separate what they call the men, which really are the boys at 10 years old and up, from the women and the other kids. They slit the throat of a young man, 27 years old. The other men panicked, started to run in every direction. The Seleka men, who were mostly men in civilians with machetes, but a few guys in uniforms with AK–47s as well, they started shooting at them and they killed four more people, including a 13-year-old boy.

The other men made it out to the bush, many of which I talked to. And when they came back at night to see what had happened, the women and the kids were gone. They could figure out from the footsteps in the sand that they had left with the anti-balaka, but they don't know what happened to them. They think they are probably dead.

The village was burned to the ground. All their cattle, which is their livelihood, was killed. Only the heads of the cows were laying on the ground.

In the same camp, I talked to another man, an older Muslim man. His name was Massadou Bichefou, and he had two wives, 11 kids and grandkids, and the same thing happened to him in early September. Anti-balaka came in. He was able to escape and hide in the grass, but he saw the anti-balaka come in, take each and every of his 11 kids and grandkids, to anti-balaka men with a knife who slit the throat of each and every of them one by one.

So, you know, what we heard when we were there was a bit new to us, the sort of new sectarian religious undertone to the violence. We did not hear that when we were in the country between March and June. And it is extremely worrying in a country like the CAR where people have lived well for many years. And it is not a country that was about religion to begin with, but people with guns on both sides seem to be using religious tensions to justify the crimes they are committing against defenseless civilians on both sides.

So what this could do to the whole country, of course, is extremely worrying. It is hard to predict. And to get a better sense of it, we ventured a bit outside of Bossangoa. We went to a small town called Zere, and the Bishop I am sure is familiar with this place. There was no one on the road. We drove for 2 hours without meeting anyone. The few women we saw alongside the road were so scared when they saw us—because they thought we were the Seleka because we had a 4x4—that they were running into the bush, dropping all their belongings, everything they had. One of them even dropped a baby on the side of the road. It took us half an hour to find the mother to take the baby back.

When we arrived in Zere, it is a very eerie feeling. It is a ghost town. The church has been burned. The mosque has been destroyed. We counted 300 burned houses there, including all of the Muslim houses. It is completely devastated.

And we spent a bit of time there and eventually some men came out of the bush. They were carrying spears and machetes, old guns, knives. They told us they were not anti-balaka, and they described the Seleka violence. When we asked them about the burned Muslim houses, they said they did not know what happened. And they told us about the kind of lives they live now. They live in the bush, three kilometers out in the bush. The kids are dying of malaria. The women are giving birth under trees, and they are getting absolutely no aid whatsoever. People in Bossangoa have a bit of aid; these people do not.

So to conclude now, you know, what could the U.S. Government do to prevent the country from spiraling further into chaos? First, I think the U.S. should support the deployment of a U.N. peacekeeping mission. I think it would be a mistake to put all your eggs in the MISCA basket, in the African force basket. I saw them on the ground. There are too few of them. They are ill-equipped and not very professional. They provide private security for money in Bangui, in Bossangoa. They get pushed around by the Seleka. They sell beer and bottled water. Put simply, I think they are not up to the task.

Now, they are the only game in town for now, and it is true that the U.N. peacekeeping mission will take some time to deploy. But I think, Mr. Chairman, you were right to say that preparations for that could start right now with no real downside to this.

And I believe that in places like Zere or Bossangoa a few blue helmets, a few professional peacekeepers, would provide enough security that people would go back to their homes, rebuild, cultivate their fields, and restart their lives.

Second point, the humanitarian aid, I believe the U.S. could provide much more. The needs are staggering, and the people, especially living in the bush, are getting absolutely nothing and dying of diseases that could be easily treated.

A third point, I think the U.S. could start sanctioning some of the people who are committing the worst abuses there, including Seleka leaders. Some of them are starting to get real access to a natural resource, to money, and they would care. And the U.S. should push the U.N. to do exactly the same thing.

Right now, there is complete impunity for these crimes. Sanctions would not be the perfect solution, but at least it would signal that there is a cost for these abuses.

So thank you very much, Mr. Chairman, and of course I am happy to answer any of your questions.

[The prepared statement of Mr. Bolopion follows:]

HRW.org

Testimony of Philippe Bolopion
United Nations Director, Human Rights Watch
Crisis in the Central African Republic
Subcommittee on Africa, Global Health,
Global Human Rights, and International Organizations
November 19, 2013

Mr. Chairman, Ranking Member Bass, thank you for inviting me to testify today. I am so pleased that this subcommittee is turning its attention to the Central African Republic – a country that often gets little attention but is at a point of crisis that demands urgent and immediate engagement by the international community – and the United States.

I came back from the Central African Republic, a landlocked and deeply impoverished country in central Africa, less than two weeks ago. I spent a week in the country on a mission for Human Rights Watch, an international human rights organization.

I arrived in the capital, Bangui, carrying piles of our latest report. It is 79 pages long, and a brutal read. It covers the period from March to June of this year and details the killing of scores of civilians, including women and children, by members of the Seleka rebels, now in power. It also documents the destruction of entire villages.

As bad as I knew the situation was, it did not prepare me for what we found on the ground. We spent several days in Bossangoa, a town of 40,000 inhabitants, 300 kilometers north of Bangui. At the entrance to the town, we found a checkpoint manned by young former Seleka fighters. They were wearing flip-flops, random uniforms, and were carrying old weapons – all trademarks of the now nominally disbanded force.

Yet they rule the town, or what is left of it. Close to 40,000 people are living around the church in one of the worst ad-hoc displaced persons camps I have seen. It reeks of human waste and is filled with bitter smoke and dust. Only a handful of non-governmental organizations and UN agencies provide help.

Many of these people have houses still standing, only a few hundred yards away. They were not displaced by a natural catastrophe, but by fear. They told us that whenever they venture out of the camp, Seleka fighters shoot at them.

Resident after resident told me of losing loved ones to Seleka bullets in their fields or houses. I met Florence Namngafo, a woman roughly my age, carrying a baby with a nasty wound. Her husband was killed by the same Seleka bullet that almost took her baby's arm. She survived by playing dead for hours, unable to assist her infant, who was screaming in pain.

A few hundred yards away, around 4,000 displaced Muslims residents are living in the long-since-closed school and court building. They fled attacks not by the Seleka, which is predominantly Muslim, but by mostly Christian armed groups commonly referred to as "anti-balaka," which means anti-machete. These local groups were activated in reaction to months of ruthless Seleka abuses.

While these mostly Christian armed groups define their purpose as self-defense against Seleka abuses, they have themselves often espoused radical anti-Muslim rhetoric and carried out deadly attacks against Muslim civilians. Such attacks have sometimes been carried out in coordination with better-armed former army elements that remain loyal to former President François Bozizé and seek his return to power.

According to the stories I heard, the anti-balaka groups can be as cruel and abusive as the enemy they purport to defend themselves against.

Massadou Bichefou, an older man with a damaged eye, told me how anti-balaka fighters came to his house at 5 a.m. on a day in early September. He is from a Peuhl community, Muslim nomadic cattle herders. Some of the fighters were dressed in civilian clothing with primitive weapons, he said, while others were in uniform, carrying AK47 rifles. He was able to escape in the dense bush but says he saw the aggressors bring each and every one of his 11 children and grandchildren to a man with a knife, who slit their throats, one by one. The youngest was 8 months old. His two wives met the same fate. He held his tears as he spelled the name and age of every lost one. Some of the attackers, he said, were former neighbors.

Other Peuhl people described how their village was attacked a month ago, also at 5 a.m., by a similar group of anti-balaka who arrived announcing that they wanted to "exterminate all the Muslims." They separated the men and older boys from the women and the other children. Seydou Hiroyi, who survived, told me that he saw anti-balaka men slit the throat of his 27-year-old brother.

When he and the other men fled in panic, the militiamen opened fire, killing three more people, including a 13-year-old boy.

Seydou and a few other men came back at night. All they found were footprints suggesting the women and children had left with the anti-balaka. He is convinced they are all dead. The houses had been looted and burned, and the cattle killed, with only the heads of the animals left on the ground.

Many people we talked to described the conflict in sectarian terms, with Muslims attacking Christians, and Christians attacking Muslims. This was something we had never heard before during research trips to the Central African Republic. It is particularly worrying in a country where both communities have always lived well together, and where the crisis had little to do with religion to begin with. But for months, even though they didn't always spare Muslim communities, Seleka fighters, who are in overwhelming numbers Muslims, targeted Christian communities with particular viciousness, often looting and destroying churches. This did not go over well with the large Christian majority in the country. Today, those carrying the guns on both sides and committing abuses on defenseless civilians seem eager to exploit religious tensions to their advantage. Though they rarely face off, they attack each other's perceived communities with abandon.

What this could do to the Central African Republic is extremely worrying, but hard to predict. To get an idea, we ventured out of the relative safety of Bossangoa to a village called Zéré, down the road to the east. During the few hours we drove on a dirt road, we never saw another vehicle, nor a Seleka fighter. Yet all the villages along the road are deserted. And the few women we encountered on the way ran into the bush in fear for their lives at the sound of our vehicle, dropping all their belongings on the road.

Zéré is now an eerie ghost town. The cycle of Seleka attacks on Christians, anti-balaka attacks against Muslims, followed by Seleka reprisals, have left the town in ruins. The church was charred, the Mosque destroyed and the chief of the Muslim neighborhood killed. We counted 300 burned houses. The school and health center have been completely looted. We talked to a few men who eventually came out of the bush carrying spears, machetes and knives. They live with their families a few kilometers back in the jungle. They told us of their children dying of Malaria and their wives giving birth under trees. No one is helping these people, mainly because of the lack of security and the difficulty reaching them. They told us about the Seleka attacks but claimed to be unaware of what had happened to their Muslim neighbors.

Back in Bangui, I met with the country's interim president, and former Seleka leader, Michel Djotodia. He received me not in the Presidential palace, but in a military camp on a hill in Bangui, in a blacked-out office with omnipresent security cameras. He was open and claimed that he was trying to bring some abusive ex-Seleka commanders under control. But he also tried to downplay the abuses Seleka forces have been responsible for, and at times seemed out of touch with the dangers facing his country.

I also met with the security minister, Pastor Josué Binoua, formerly loyal to Bozizé, the ousted president. He told me that he only had 110 weapons for the 4,500 gendarmes and 1,400 policemen under his command.

I sat down with one of the former Seleka strongmen, and now head of intelligence, Noureddine Adam, who has been accused by Reporters Without Borders, a press freedom organization, of threatening journalists. He too downplayed the abuses described in many harrowing details in our report.

I was left with the impression that no one is really at the helm, and that the country could easily spin out of control.

The religious leaders I met at the national level seemed to be the only ones struggling to keep the country together. The archbishop of Bangui, Dieudonné Nzapalainga, and Imam Omar Kobine Layama are both fully aware of the danger created by sectarian tensions. Both work together to condemn, at great risk to their safety, the abuses committed against civilians of all sides. But they do not control the men with the guns.

So what could be done to prevent the country from spiraling into chaos, with untold numbers of lives claimed in the process?

For now, the international community has placed all its chips on an ill-equipped and ill-trained African peacekeeping mission of 2,500 troops called MICOPAX, initially deployed as a sub-regional force by the Economic Community of Central African States. On December 19, it is supposed to transfer its authority to MISCA, an African Union-led force relying on many of the same countries to supply troops, with a planned strength of 3,652.

Without these peacekeepers, the country would probably be in complete anarchy. Only their presence brought back a measure of security in Bangui, or, for example, in the displaced camps of Bossangoa.

But they are not up to the task. In Bangui they rarely patrol the streets and supplement their income by providing private security to businesses and rich individuals. In Bossangoa they sell beer and get pushed around by the Seleka whenever they try to venture outside of the town.

We believe that they should be urgently reinforced by a UN peacekeeping mission of the type that has been successfully deployed in Ivory Coast or Liberia. A few thousand professional and well-equipped blue helmets could deploy throughout the country, in places like Bossangoa or Zéré. With a strong mandate to protect civilians, they would keep the armed men in check, and provide enough security that people could leave the camps and the bush and come back to their villages. They could start rebuilding their houses, cultivating their fields, tend to their cattle, and learn to live together again.

The UN is ready to undertake a peacekeeping mission, with a strong human rights monitoring section, and the US could use its seat in the Security Council to help make it happen. There would be a cost to the US, but it's a worthy investment. The human rights situation is dire, and yet it could get much worse, engulfing the entire region and creating a failed state many armed groups will be eager to exploit. A UN peacekeeping mission could help protect civilians and avert the worst, while it is still possible.

In the interim, there are three things the US should do while it actively works to secure a UN peacekeeping force.

First, the US should do more to support the current AU force on the ground – both diplomatically and technically – to ensure it is, at a minimum, regularly patrolling the streets and where possible, providing some measure of protection for civilians who have nowhere else to turn. Although the US has been a vocal supporter of the need for greater civilian protection in the Central African Republic, it has not allocated any funds for peacekeeping.

Second, the US could expand its humanitarian assistance in the Central African Republic. In late September, the US provided $11.5 million for refugees who fled to neighboring countries, while in response to the dramatically deteriorating humanitarian situation a total of roughly $17 million has been allocated for those suffering at the hands of Seleka and anti-Balaka forces, including $8.2 million in emergency programs and $8.8 million in food assistance in FY 2013. According to the UN, half of the population needs help. Although this is one of the worst situations in the world, it's also grossly underfunded.

Finally, the US could sanction those most responsible for human rights abuses, including Seleka leaders, with visa bans and asset freezes. It may be unlikely that these individuals actually have assets in the United States or intend to travel here but such a step would nonetheless make an important contribution toward accountability. The US could also work with other members of the UN Security Council to push for similar global UN sanctions against these individuals, to help raise the cost of abuses and seek to interrupt the cycle of violence.

Thank you Mr. Chairman, I'm happy to answer your questions.

Mr. SMITH. Mr. Bolopion, thank you very much for your recommendations, your work on the ground as well.

Because I know she does have to leave, I would like to yield to my friend and colleague, Ms. Bass, for questions.

Ms. BASS. Thank you very much, Mr. Chairman.

Following up from each of your comments, I wanted to know, since each of you have been there recently, do you see U.S. assistance on the ground? Do you see evidence of it? And what type of assistance do you see? And maybe each of you could comment briefly to that.

Mr. BOLOPION. Maybe I will go first. No, I did not see any U.S. assistance, though I was not engaged in delivery of any humanitarian aid, so I wouldn't take this as a probing sign.

Mr. JOBBINS. From our end, we are supported by USAID and Catholic Relief——

Ms. BASS. You receive funding from——

Mr. JOBBINS. We are supported to respond to the needs of communities in the southeast of the country, which is not this area that has been most affected as of yet. We understand that there are discussions about additional U.S. assistance to a number of actors in the country, but I don't know the status of those beyond the current programs that we have had since before this current crisis.

Ms. BASS. Have you had assistance to go into other areas? Do you have the capacity to do that?

Mr. JOBBINS. Yes, we do. And many of the humanitarian organizations on the ground do have the capacity to respond to almost every one of these needs. There are health actors, there are food security actors, there are peace and conflict resolution organizations. So there is the capacity to respond. It is, at the moment, of mobilizing resources and ensuring a modicum of security to begin operating.

Ms. BASS. Bishop?

Bishop NONGO-AZIAGBIA. The American Embassy in the Central African Republic has closed down long time ago. I would say there is no American presence as such in the Central African Republic, and the American Government made a statement calling all its citizens to come back to the States or not to travel to the Central African Republic.

But so far as I know, there is Catholic Relief Services, which is present in the Central African Republic working in Bangui, in the eastern part of the Central African Republic in the region where the LRA are operating.

In the crisis we are living in Bossangoa since the 8th of September, the first humanitarian assistance we received it was through CRS.

Thank you.

Ms. BASS. So I want to ask you, in general, the panel, a question—if you can provide options and suggestions for ways in which the U.S. Government could best support civil society in the Republic. But then I am not exactly sure to what extent civil society is functioning, so maybe you could respond to both accounts.

Bishop NONGO-AZIAGBIA. To the best of my knowledge, the best way of helping the civil society in the Central African Republic, it will be through American organizations such as CRS. They have a foot on the ground. They know the reality. They can help efficiently, monitoring any funds coming from the American Government.

Mr. JOBBINS. To our perspective, there is certainly a role for civil society and for all sorts of actors in responding to the crisis, not just the formal civil society human rights groups that have been involved in documenting the abuses and in lobbying against them, but also church leaders, media organizations.

We have seen the work that the bishops have been doing with the imams in a number of cities to reduce tensions and begin establishing relationships, and to break down some of those rumors and fears. At the same time, there is a need to take that work to scale.

There are only so many people you can have in a meeting room as you sort of talk through these issues. And so what happens is the events in Bossangoa, for example, when people hear of that elsewhere in the country that creates fear throughout the entire country because of the events that are happening there. And the good work that is being done isn't necessarily getting out.

So when people turn on their radios, they listen to the Radio Centrafrique, they listen to the atrocities that are being committed, they listen to news or rumors and fear that spread, but there isn't any opportunity for people to carve out another solution. And so media can play a key role in promoting that, in both managing rumors and also promoting moderate voices, promoting non-violent voices, recognizing that everyone, every Central African, is deeply upset by what they are seeing happen to their country.

But there is this choice that young people have to make. Do you join—you know, if you are young and afraid of your own personal safety, do you choose to align yourself with an anti-balaka group, or align yourself with a different kind of armed group? Or do you choose to engage with the people who you are fearing from, so that you are developing a way to protect yourself as a community?

And ultimately that is the choice that everyone has to make, and yet it is not something that is being discussed, or it is not something that is being actively supported. And so there is a huge opportunity to support religious groups, but to support human rights groups, youth organizations, media organizations, to start having that conversation and supporting the people who are making that choice, to protect and look out for their community in a way that doesn't necessarily lead the country further down the road to chaos.

Ms. BASS. Yes. And people need a third alternative, obviously. And I know you are talking about international organizations, and maybe you are talking about domestic organizations, because I was in terms of, what is the capacity on the ground of domestic organizations. And maybe you could follow with both questions.

Mr. BOLOPION. Yeah. You know, I would say the number one issue right now is security. If you are a human rights activist, even in Bangui today, if you are a journalist you ought to fear for your life. And so that climate makes it very difficult for anyone to operate freely in the country.

And journalists recently have been interrogated by Noureddine Adam, who is the head of intelligence in the country. I spoke with the highest-ranking imam in the country, Imam Kobine. He told me that only a few weeks ago he received death threats from a high-ranking person in the government with the rank of minister.

So as long as you have this kind of climate, and as long as you have men with guns doing whatever they please in Bangui and in the rest of the country, it will be very hard to allow civil society to really flourish.

Ms. BASS. And when you were describing the religious violence, you were describing it on both sides, I believe, Christians to Muslims, Muslims to Christians?

Mr. BOLOPION. Absolutely. I think the tragedy right now is that you have in the country two armed groups, the Seleka who are in power, the anti-balaka, mostly Christian militias, and they almost never fight each other, or it is very rare. What they do is attack civilians, defenseless civilians, with brutality from communities they believe are associated with their enemies.

So the Seleka will attack the Christian population of a village. The anti-balaka will retaliate against the Muslim population of the same village. The Seleka will come back to punish the Christian population for this attack. So both groups, as far as we can tell, are using the same brutal and bloody tactics.

Ms. BASS. And I believe that the three of you had a difference in terms of whether or not the U.S. should appoint a special advisor, special envoy. I wanted to know if you could respond to that, and then I just have one more question after that, Mr. Chair.

Mr. BOLOPION. Maybe I will go first, then. It is not a recommendation we have made so far, but I believe any measure that would elevate this issue in U.S. foreign policy and bring it higher level attention would be beneficial. The Central African Republic for a long time has suffered from being ignored. Most people would not be able to place it on a map.

So anything that can start changing that, given the urgency of the situation on the ground, would be positive, I believe.

Mr. JOBBINS. From our end, we do work closely with the special advisor, who was here earlier, who is in the State Department. Our view from the ground would be as soon as possible to reopen the Embassy and to have a full diplomatic presence, to engage in these very sensitive questions and to monitor, of course, the assistance that hopefully will be provided.

But at the same time, what we are also asking is for increased visibility, increased public statements, increased awareness from within Central African Republic, that this is an issue that the U.S. is looking—is watching, is caring about. We have seen several cases where international lobbying, international concerns, about crimes being committed, about the responsibility of certain Seleka commanders for committing crimes, has yielded real change on the ground in terms of, you know, people being rescinded from various posts because of international support, international recognition.

And so the more that the U.S. publicly engages, it can only have positive results for the people in the Central African Republic.

Ms. BASS. Thank you.

Bishop NONGO-AZIAGBIA. I don't believe personally that the American Government could make much difference or much change in the situation on the ground in the Central African Republic from

Washington. We need to get people on the ground to live the experience the Central African people are going through.

Also, a delegation from the U.N. security visited Bossangoa. They came by plane, spent 6 hours within the city of Bossangoa. Prior to their visit, means were taken for their safety, for their protection. Troops were sent in from Bangui, while the people living in Bossangoa, they don't have such security.

I made that clear to the U.N. assistant in matter of security. If you want to have a feel of what the people are living, experiencing, don't stay within the city of Bossangoa. Get out of that city at a radius of 25 kilometers. Things will be different from your own perspective.

So from this office, from our office in Washington, we will be talking, but we won't be feeling what the people are living in the Central African Republic.

Thank you.

Ms. BASS. And my last question to you, Bishop, the Principal Deputy Assistant Secretary—that is a mouthful—mentioned that there was the potential for elections in 2015. And based on everything that we have heard today, how on earth could elections be held in 2015? I mean, do you see parties formed? Are there candidates that are trying to garner support? What is your thoughts on whether or not the nation would be ready for national elections in 2015?

Bishop NONGO-AZIAGBIA. I would say it is possible that elections might be fairly conducted in 2015, if all the conditions for security are guaranteed into the country by sending in MISCA troops or whichever troops, but with specific mandate to bring in peace.

I would like just to give you a testimony from the call I had with my vicar general early this morning. At exactly 3:29 a.m., I called my vicar general just to have the latest news from Bossangoa. The news he gave me was really threatening, because the city of Bossangoa, as for now, has been surrounded by the Seleka elements, the increased number in that city.

So you can't travel outside of Bossangoa. Bossangoa is, I will say, a big open prison. So on one direction the Seleka killed five—they came across a group of five young men, killed three, dropped their bodies into a river. Two managed to escape and then run to the Catholic Church for their lives. On the other direction, they came across the anti-balaka militia groups. They fought, there are lots of human loss, of death.

As they returned back to Bossangoa, they surrounded the Catholic mission with the over 35,000 people displaced there, threatening to shoot at them. So this night the people in the Catholic Church compound didn't sleep. That was the message I received.

I called the Minister of Security and Internal Affairs, asking him to react, and the response he gave me was a pathetic answer because his life is threatened. He has been accused of plotting against Djotodia and his regime, because he is telling him the truth. And those surrounding Djotodia don't want the change. That is where we are coming to. They came. They want to stick to the power, and they will use all means at their disposal to stick themselves into power.

Mr. SMITH. Bishop Nongo, let me ask you, so right now, as you testify, the people that you are trying to protect are under siege, surrounded by people with weapons. What does MISCA do? Do they in any way deploy? What is the response? How many people are surrounding the compound?

Bishop NONGO-AZIAGBIA. Presently, MISCA is not in existence because the decision will be taken hopefully in December. We have presently the MICOPAX operating in the Central African Republic, but MICOPAX is helpless.

There are, from my perspective, observers of all the abuses committed on the population, against the population. They are there to see that you are killed in a proper way, and then maybe take the news abroad.

We have a group of about 60 or 80 MICOPAX elements based in Bossangoa to protect over 35,000 people displaced at the Catholic Church. There is an average of 12 or 15 men posted there. There are three who are posted at the school where the Muslim displaced people are. It is not enough. We want the deployment of a U.N. force in that country to better protect the population.

Mr. SMITH. I know, Mr. Jobbins, you in your testimony talked about that prior to MISCA's deployment—and of course I understand that they are not deployed—that there is a heightened sense—I mean, a dangerous situation seems to be even more dangerous, if that is possible, because they are not there, and yet the bad guys know that they are coming.

Would all of you agree that a U.N. force, blue helmets, with a Chapter VII mandate, is required in this situation? Otherwise, we might see a false hope and expectation that MISCA can bring about protection. I mean, those were the Bishop's comments to my staff and I when we met several months ago.

You know, if we haven't learned that lesson yet, that you have got to have the right force, or else there is a dooming to failure. As a matter of fact, I was struck in your testimony, Bishop Nongo, when you pointed out that there is a de facto occupation occurring in the CAR, a foreign occupation at that. People from the outside actually have pretty much invaded your country, and I don't think that is as appreciated as it ought to be.

So if you could speak, if you all would, to—I mean, I am thinking that what this subcommittee will do, at least I will and I am sure I will be joined by other members, would be to write to the administration along the lines of the questions that I suggested to the Ambassador earlier, that there is nothing to preclude simultaneously working to get this, you know, under U.N. auspices and also with a much more serious mandate. And certainly Chapter VII mandates are the best.

Mr. BOLOPION. If I may comment on that, Mr. Chairman. I mean, I think there is no question that right now the African troops are the only game in town. They are the only ones on the ground, and if they were not there the situation would probably be much worse.

Now, is that enough to face the challenges the country is facing? Absolutely not. The Bishop described the numbers of troops in Bossangoa. I saw them. I have seen peacekeepers in other countries. They patrol. They have armored vehicles. They have a sort of aggressive stance, and they are ready to confront anyone who is antagonizing civilians.

This is not the case in Bossangoa. At one point when we were leaving the cities for these day trips to see villages around, there was a crew of foreign journalists that wanted to come with us with an escort from the FOMAC, the African peacekeeping mission there. And we didn't have any escort. We were allowed to go through the Seleka checkpoints. The BBC were authorized, but the FOMAC patrol was stopped by the Seleka, and they just went back to their base.

So they are not ready to confront the bad guys there. And so what to do about it? I think they need to be supported right now, and I think the $40 million that could be put to that are probably a great thing.

But you need to start running right now for a U.N. peacekeeping mission. Yesterday, the U.N. gave to Security Council members very good detailed reports giving options for how the international community could help with the situation. And the options ranged to very minimal support to MISCA all the way to a full-blown U.N. peacekeeping mission of the type that you have in the Democratic Republic of the Congo, in Liberia, in Ivory Coast, for example. These will be blue helmets. They would be certainly not the perfect solution, but they would be much more professional than what we have right now.

They would have more vehicles, communications, command. They would have a civilian component of the mission that could work on justice, elections, security, things like that. So the U.N. is ready to do it. There is a good report on the table, and I think the U.S. should consider it in a very positive light.

Another offer that the U.N. Secretary-General made is to say, ''Look, it is a very urgent situation. Things could go really bad. You could give us the authorization to redeploy U.N. peacekeepers from neighboring countries to intervene in the country if it comes to that.'' I think it is also something that should be looked at very carefully.

Mr. SMITH. Excellent point. Before we go to Mr. Jobbins, you know, one of the biggest takeaways from Srebrenica—and I have been there for reinterment of some 800 bodies when about 8,000 Muslims were slaughtered in the course of about a week—was that the peacekeepers, they were all about force protection, not civilian protection, and we have seen that replicated time and time again.

And, as you pointed out in that conversation about how the peacekeepers were turned away and went back to their barracks, I mean, if that doesn't underscore and illustrate, you know, a deficiency, I don't know what does. So thank you for that.

Mr. Jobbins.

Mr. JOBBINS. From our end, we don't have any particular insight into whether a U.N. or African Union peacekeeping force is the most effective. But our position in evaluating the different plans, and certainly the ones that were put forward by the U.N. Secretary-General yesterday, the questions that we have to ask ourselves is, the speed of deployment, how can we get the most troops on the ground fast with the mandate that they require?

Those, as far as we are concerned, are the only criteria. And which international administrative body it falls under is less important than the speed, the numbers, and the mandate that they have, and the degree of mobility.

What is important to understand is that we have a very tragic situation in Bossangoa. We have dozens of other cities where there are almost as tense situations, and so the peacekeeping force needs to have the mandate and the troop strength to be able to cover a very large space the size of Texas that is sparsely populated and where, because of the climate of fear, conflict and tensions can erupt relatively quickly in a number of different places. And so mobility and geographical coverage is important.

Mr. SMITH. Are the troops contemplated under MISCA adequate?

Mr. JOBBINS. The troops contemplated under MISCA, I believe under the latest, it is 3,600 who are authorized, and they are looking at potentially going up to 9,000. In terms of the numbers, I am not a military planner, but they certainly need quite a lot.

And the only other component that we would add that hasn't been mentioned yet by my co-panelists, but I hope they would agree with us is also the support to BINUCA, which is the political arm, which was also recognized in Security Council Resolution 2121, and the need for sustained U.N. political engagement on human rights issues, but also if we want to see elections, we want to see these things, there needs to already be an international political accompaniment as well as the security accompaniment.

Mr. SMITH. Bishop.

Bishop NONGO-AZIAGBIA. Mr. Mueller, in his report, after the visit he made to the Central African Republic, made that statement, that the 3,600 men from the MISCA is far below what is needed on the ground. So there is a need to increase that number to 9,000 to 10,000 men, I would say. And the composition of the Council members should be also looked into.

From the perspective of the Central African people, the contribution of Chad, as stated in the crisis in the Central African Republic, has not been clear because Chad has been in a way instrumentalizing the crisis in the Central African Republic for its personal benefit.

On the economic side, in the northern part of the Central African Republic, Chad has drilled its oil. They have two wells. One of the two wells is on the Central African Republic soil. So you do understand that the continuous crisis in the Central African Republic, the insecurity, will help Chad to continue exploiting our natural resources without anybody looking at it.

We have this long troubled relationship with Chad as far as cattle herders and farmers are concerned. Chad is desert country. They need grass for their cattle. And according to international law, there is a tract made for the cattle herders, but they are not respecting this tract. They take their cattle into farmer's field, destroying the crops and everything. That has been, for the past years, source of tension between farmers from the Central African Republic and cattle herders from Chad.

So those cattle herders come with rifles, guns. They shoot at the farmers, burn down their houses, and the creation of the anti-balaka groups, it is not just a new event, because the anti-balaka groups did form since the '90s to fight the armed marauders, and then they are then fighting these cattle herders coming from Chad, destroying their crops, their villages, their houses.

Now they are fighting to protect what they call their right. So we need to look into that. The international community maybe should help the Central African Republic to sort things out with Chad.

Mr. SMITH. Bishop, thank you. I will put my remaining questions on temporary hold, because we have the privilege of being joined by the chairman of the full committee, Congressman or Chairman Ed Royce.

Chairman SMITH. Thank you. Thank you very much, Chairman.

One of the concerns that many of us had with respect to the activities of the Janjaweed when they were participating in ethnic cleansing, which they still are, in Sudan, was the spillover effect that that would have in the region. And what we have seen are the same tactics of the Janjaweed. Indeed, probably 85 percent, 90 percent of this force, is not indigenous to Central African Republic. It is coming in from Sudan. It is coming in from Chad.

And these foreign fighters have learned a particular method of operation. And what we see them doing in towns across the Central African Republic is committing the same types of looting, of rapes, of torture as well here. By the way, and their focus on going after the Catholic Church, which at this point is probably the only real institution functioning in the country, and functioning on the standpoint of not just the school systems that they deal with but also in terms of the social welfare network, in targeting a country which is 85 percent Christian and 12 percent Muslim, the other danger here is that they are going to ignite, as you are discussing, the sectarian conflict.

And just as this has expanded, you are going to have a continued arithmetic increase in the struggles between Christians—animus—Muslims, because, as the Bishop has explained, one of the consequences of this is if you are taking cattle that you have herded and you are turning it over later to a local Muslim cattle herder, then the tensions are going to be expanded to the ethnic tensions within that local community.

And the real danger here is that this is a country the size of Texas that is engulfed now. But we are seeing this MO, you know, deployed across North Africa. And the reason we are supportive of action being taken is in order to try to arrest this, we met with Samantha Power, our new Ambassador to the U.N., had a meeting with her and the committee last week, and this was the foremost issue she wanted to talk about, which is indicative of how destructive this is going to be in terms of the African continent.

I think the other aspect of this I would like to ask you about, and I will just expand this into our ongoing effort after 17 years, or whatever it has been, we finally had a pretty good operation going against Joseph Kony under legislation that we wrote. And that focus was on running Kony down, and he was in the southeast area of the Central African Republic. And all of that seemingly has been put on hold as we deal with the bigger disaster, allowing him, theoretically, to regroup, you know, to resupply.

Again, it has been problematic in the past that the Sudanese Government has supplied him. I don't know that they would continue to do that. But their tolerance of the activities of the Janjaweed, and their encouragement of it, has helped put us in this crisis today. So just some observations on those two points, if you would, and thank our panelists again.

And, Chairman, I thank you and Karen Bass for your engagement in this. And, by the way, Mr. Marino has been very involved as well, and I really think it is going to take members' engagement here in order to push up, you know, the focus on the Central African Republic and on the need to get the support there, both in terms of what we do for relief but also in terms of MISCA's efforts.

Go ahead.

Mr. JOBBINS. Thank you, Chairman Royce, and thank you for all of the work that the entire committee has been doing to bring attention to this issue. On the first question of the influx of this movement and of Seleka inflaming wider religious tensions, it is certainly a trend that we have seen and one that we are very fearful will continue to increase.

The pattern in several places, including in Bangassou and Yaloke, we have seen that when Seleka units or Seleka groups felt under attack that they sought to actively rally the local Muslim community to their cause. Many of these communities are ethnic pulled, many of them are not, from the same backgrounds of the Seleka forces.

But we see them trying to forge these alliances or trying to establish a local support base, because many of them come from far afield, they are looking to establish roots in the country and reaching out and involving Muslim communities to do so, which is triggering the back and forth reprisal attacks that we have heard of and that Bishop Nongo illustrated so well.

So that is a worrying trend. It is one that may continue as the movement continues to fracture. We have seen fighting now between Seleka groups. And as this sort of mixed group tries to devise, and continues to try and set down roots, we see risks of further attempts to mobilize civilians.

On the question of the fight against the LRA and Joseph Kony, it is true that up until this most recent violence that there had been a lot of significant progress in reducing the operational space and encouraging defections, and that was set back by this instability. It seems as though efforts are ramping up again, but it is true that there was a moment of pause in which the LRA was able to regroup.

And we are quite afraid that as the dry season sets in, there is going to be increasing trade between the remote areas that are historically targeted. And so as traders move back and forth between these cities that haven't been resupplied, first because of the fighting and then because of the rainy season, as people have to start getting food, have to start getting supplies out to these remote areas, those are new targets and new opportunities for the LRA and other armed groups to prey upon.

Chairman ROYCE. Thank you. I, again, thank the panelists, and I yield back. I know Mr. Marino has been waiting, and I also want to thank him for allowing me to go out of sequence.

But thank you, Mr. Chairman.

Mr. SMITH. One of the wonders of this committee, really of Congress, is that there are so many people of extraordinary talent. Well, Mr. Marino used to be the U.S. Attorney in Pennsylvania, so has a wealth of law enforcement knowledge, and was a very effective U.S. Attorney. He is a member of our subcommittee, and I yield to him such time as he may consume.

Mr. MARINO. Thank you, Chairman.

Gentlemen, welcome, and I apologize for being a little late. I am doing the traditional marathon here today, because of three committees simultaneously having hearings.

But I have a constituent in my district, in the 10th District of Pennsylvania. It is the north-central northeast. Actually, it is the largest district in the state. I have 15 of the 67 countries. So it is a very large geographical area.

And Jon Cassel has been working in the Central African Republic for a number of years with the Christian Broadcasting Network. And Jon has—he has an ambivalence concerning Chad, fighters from Chad going into the Central African Republic and choosing sides.

What is the U.S. doing to address Chad's role in the Central African Republic? And on top of that, what is the international community doing as well? So, Mr. Bolopion?

Mr. BOLOPION. Thank you, sir. We hear a lot of things, too, about the involvement of Chad in what is happening in the Central African Republic. We have not done extensive research on that. We do not know who is pulling the strings and who is playing what games exactly in the country. Frankly, it is very hard to follow because at times alliances are made very quickly, as fast as they are being rescinded, so it is a very complex situation.

I would say that Chad will soon join the U.N. Security Council. Starting on January 1, they will sit around the table there with the U.S., and they will have a major say in decisions the U.N. Security Council will take about the situation in the Central African Republic, including for the deployment of a U.N. peacekeeping mission, if it comes to that.

So I think your question is extremely relevant, and I believe that the presence of Chad around the table will provide the U.S. Government with ample opportunities to ask tough questions to the Chadian diplomats there.

Thank you.

Mr. MARINO. I am going to shift gears here a little bit, and then if you gentlemen would like to respond to any of the questions when I get through these. I only have 5 minutes.

Thank you, Chairman.

It has been brought to my attention—and I would like to know if you can verify this for me, any one of you could verify this for me—the USAID has been reluctant to work with religious-based organizations throughout the world, which is especially harmful in the Central African Republic.

As the chairman keenly alluded to, the Catholic Church is probably one of the last humanitarian organizations still functioning in the Central African Republic. Is that the case? Are any of you finding out that USAID is reluctant to work with the Catholic Church?

Bishop, this sounds like this is right in your area.

Bishop NONGO-AZIAGBIA. I don't really know the policy governing the way the American Government is working, and then disbursing its help or assistance, humanitarian assistance, to which organizations, I can't really see, because I haven't been working with the American Government, neither benefitting from any assistance from them.

But the only thing I know is when the crisis really broke up in Bossangoa, the first emergency assistance we received it was through CRS, which is a faith-based organization, an American faith-based organization. Where do they get their money? I guess from the American Government.

Mr. MARINO. Okay. I want to make——

Mr. SMITH. Would the gentleman yield on that?

Mr. MARINO. Yes, please.

Mr. SMITH. In part, but in large part, very often it is raised through other sources as well. So I did ask the Ambassador when he testified, Ambassador Jackson, if he could give us a full accounting as to how much money has been let to faith-based organizations. And I pointed out my deep disappointment, having just returned from Nigeria, when I discovered, really to my shock, that despite having ample capability and capacity the church was largely overlooked, and just 9 percent of our PEPFAR money and health dollars were going to faith-based organizations. And I am talking about mostly indigenous, on-the-ground infrastructure and capacity that was being overlooked.

Mr. MARINO. And thank you for bringing that point up, because Jon, my constituent who spends a lot of time there, you know, brought this to my attention. And we need to do more work, Chairman, to see that funds are, how can we say it, fairly disbursed, because the Catholic organization and my mother—I hope she is listening, because I am a Roman Catholic, and my mother wanted me to be a priest, and it just didn't work out that way. So she would be proud of me right now, I am hoping. But we will work hard in that direction.

Either Mr. Jobbins or Mr. Bolopion, do you have an opinion on that that you would like to make?

Mr. JOBBINS. What I can say, we work—we are not a faith-based organization, but we work very closely with Catholic Relief Services in the southeast of the Central African Republic, and that is supported by USAID. In terms of how much they are supporting in the rest of the country, I am not sure, but what I can certainly say is echo the sentiments that you have said and that the religious leaders do have a huge capacity to respond to the crisis, both religious media, religious clerics, and other sort of faith-linked organizations, both on the Christian as well as on the Muslim side, to respond to the crisis in the CAR.

Mr. MARINO. Okay.

Mr. BOLOPION. We have no expertise in this question.

Mr. MARINO. What do we do, then? What more can we do, aside from funding? How do we get the best bang for our buck? And what changes, if either—any one of you gentlemen could instantly make a change, where would it be, the change, and how would you do it? So if you each would respond to that, please.

Mr. BOLOPION. If I may, it may be on how to get the best bang for the buck. I am convinced that that would be by supporting a U.N. peacekeeping mission. I am convinced that in a place like Bossangoa, a few well-equipped, well-trained professional U.N. peacekeepers would go a long way.

We are not in a country where you are facing a real military threat. I described the Seleka men in Bossangoa. They go around in flipflops. The anti-balaka are often people carrying knives and spears. So you are not confronting on either side well-organized, well-equipped military groups. A few U.N. peacekeepers in Bossangoa and you could have 40,000 people go back to their houses, go back to their fields, the humanitarian crisis would be averted.

So I think it is the most cost-effective way for the U.S. to invest in this crisis.

Mr. JOBBINS. From our end, I think the two things to guarantee bang for the buck, the first is that a stitch in time saves nine, and that we are seeing—the failure to act today is going to lead to a much worse situation tomorrow, both in terms of funding and in terms of lives lost.

We are at a point where there are, in Bossangoa and other places, have already been tragedies, but in much of the country there have been tensions, there have been signs of danger, signs of tragedy, that haven't happened yet. And so now is an opportunity to respond quickly to keep that from coming into place.

And the second, of course, is to build on the capacity that is in place, there are humanitarian organizations. There is 28 national/international aid agencies who are working there. There are churches; there are networks in place. They can be mobilized quickly. And so there is an opportunity to respond fairly effectively and quickly.

And then, in terms of the question of the one thing that would change, we would say that alongside the support to an international peacekeeping mission is to support community non-violence actions, supporting churches, supporting media, supporting things that can begin shifting this tide, using the capacities and the initiatives and the energies that already exist among hundreds of organizations across the Central African Republic.

Mr. MARINO. Bishop, please.

Bishop NONGO-AZIAGBIA. I will just make three small points. First, peace—building peace; second, humanitarian assistance; and, third, security by supporting MISCA.

Mr. MARINO. Are there individuals—or I am seeing that there are individuals, but maybe you have a different twist on this, gentlemen, that need to be arrested and criminally prosecuted?

Bishop NONGO-AZIAGBIA. Well, from experience, and then coming across people on the ground, I will say we may produce a list of people who have been involved in the human atrocities and others. But human rights organizations have done a good job on that. I think they might help us.

Mr. BOLOPION. Thank you, Bishop. Yes, absolutely, and large numbers. The type of crimes that have been committed in the country since March are simply horrendous. Scores of people have been killed.

I described the way armed groups have slit the throats of children, so there should be a lot of people right now who should be prosecuted for these crimes, all the way up the chain, if that chain can be reconstituted. It is not happening for a very simple reason; it is that the men in power, which in some cases condone the abuses, are also controlling now the justice system, which is completely broken down.

So the only way you will bring back some measure of accountability could be through the International Criminal Court, which is closely observing the situation in the country and could decide at some point to start investigations. There could be, through the U.N. Security Council, for example, the creation of a Commission of Inquiry, which could start documenting these abuses and start looking at how we can hold these people accountable.

And as I said earlier, one thing the U.S. Government can do right now is when they have sufficient information, and the information is out there against some of these individuals who are responsible for these crimes, to sanction them and ask the U.N. to do the very same thing.

If some of these people in power right now cannot travel abroad anymore, cannot have bank accounts in other countries, cannot engage in business, for example, profiting from the natural resources they have access to right now, that will be a game-changer for them. So I think it is a very simple, very little cost measure that the U.S. could take that would really help.

Mr. MARINO. And if the chairman would just allow me one other question. I know that the United Nations has the wherewithal, it has the money, it has the people there that could do just exactly what you described, but do you think the U.N. actually has the desire to do this in Central African Republic?

Mr. BOLOPION. If we talk about the U.N. Secretary-General, the answer is yes. The U.N. Secretary-General, Ban Ki-moon, gave a report to the U.N. Security Council yesterday. This was the result of a mission that was on the ground for 2 weeks. The Bishop described talking to some members of the mission. I did as well. They were there to evaluate what the best options were.

When you read their report, I believe it is pretty clear that they think the best option would be a U.N. peacekeeping mission that would take over the African Union peacekeeping mission as quickly as possible. They know how to do this. They have done it in many countries. It is not always a perfect solution. We all have in mind very well-known failures of blue helmets in the past.

But personally, coming back from the country, having seen on the ground what the African Union mission looks like, I have very little confidence that they will be able to face the challenges ahead, including the possibility of further mass atrocities in the country.

So are they ready to do it? Yes, they are. All they need is a green light from the U.N. Security Council, and the U.S. could make that happen tomorrow.

Mr. MARINO. Thanks.

Bishop NONGO-AZIAGBIA. I will say everybody knows exactly what to do. A lot of reports have been produced about it. But up to now, I don't know why but no action is being taken. I think it is time you stop talking and then you start acting.

Mr. MARINO. I agree. Gentlemen, thank you very much. Thank you for your service.

And, Chairman, thank you for allowing me the extra time.

Mr. SMITH. Thank you. And, Mr. Marino, I would ask for your help on this as well. You know, it is my understanding that the Catholic Relief Services' work in northeast CAR is completely and totally privately funded, only the work in the southeast with regards to the LRA is not, and then it is only in part supported by USAID.

And one of the things we asked Ambassador Jackson earlier, I asked him, I think we need to do a better job in getting the money where its utilization can immediately be felt by people who are suffering hunger and medical needs.

I mean, Bishop Nongo, you are caring for 35,00 people. How are you doing it? I am sure the camps would be much nicer if you had the capability and the wherewithal, and USAID has that. And so part of the reason for this hearing as well was to try to say, ''Get the money to those individual groups that can really have an impact on the ground.'' And certainly the faith community has that capacity, and it is not being utilized.

Mr. Jobbins, would you want to——

Mr. JOBBINS. Just to send that spirit that there is a whole number of groups that can use money and can use it well to both respond to the emerging humanitarian needs, and also to prevent this cycle of violence, because there are people who are unhappy, there are people who can do things about it. It is about making sure that they have a voice and have an opportunity to start mobilizing alternatives to this kind of violence that we are seeing.

Mr. SMITH. In your statement, Mr. Jobbins, your final bottom line was this is a critical moment for the U.S. Government to engage proactively and decisively to protect civilians and prevent current threats from evolving into large scale atrocities in Central African Republic. Are we? I mean, are we really seizing the moment, or is it still something that awaits action?

Mr. JOBBINS. We have been very pleased to see the attention that is beginning to be paid to this situation. It is something, of course, we wished that there had been more attention earlier, but we are very pleased through efforts like this hearing, through some of the meetings that are going on at State and USAID to begin bringing a response. But the speed that is needed is something that we can't underestimate. It is something that we need to move. The situation gets worse every single day, and we need to move quickly.

Mr. SMITH. You said, Mr. Jobbins, in your testimony there are persistent rumors, though no confirmation, of attempts by Seleka groups to form alliances with groups from North Africa and the Middle East. Could you elaborate that? Are we talking about al-Qaeda, Boko Haram, al Shabaab? Of course, that is, in Somalia. And where does Seleka get its arms from? Have any of those arms been traced to Libya and the fall of Ghadafi?

Mr. JOBBINS. From my end, I can say what I said in my testimony, which is that there are persistent rumors. There are rumors of all sorts, including the rumors of weapons from Libya and other places abroad. What I need to emphasize is, of course, they are rumors, but they are widespread and it has been since the beginning of Seleka that there have been these kinds of rumors. And every group that you have named has been rumored to be attached to Seleka one way or another.

What we can say is that as Seleka's internal coherency weakens, as we see them feeling under military threat, and reaching out and mobilizing local, trying to mobilize local divisions to build a support base in-country, it is fair to imagine that they are trying to use this narrative of religious conflict, or that they would have this opportunity to use this narrative of religious conflict to mobilize support outside of the country as well.

Mr. SMITH. Bishop.

Bishop NONGO-AZIAGBIA. I would like to add to this answer. The borders with Chad and Sudan are a porous border. Anybody can come in and out of the country as he or she wishes, when it wishes, and there is no control. From some information, there are arms manufacturers in Sudan, AK arms in Sudan, and then people easily get arms in that area.

So it is possible that these militias, either from Chad or either from Sudan, get their arms from Sudan into the Central African Republic. The fact is, the Central African Army didn't fight the Seleka. They kept on running. As running, most of the arms are located to them for the protection of the civilians. They left it behind, and then the Seleka, as they moved, they picked whatever was left behind by the Army.

And we have some arms bought by the oustered President, kept in his own village of Benzambe, in various places in Bangui. Those arms were not used, and then the Seleka easily got access to those arms. That is what they are using.

Mr. BOLOPION. And I would just say we don't have any conclusive evidence on the issues you mention. I would say, as the U.S. weighs its options in the region, that many of the groups you mention are often attracted to countries that are lawless, and where they can operate freely, and the Central African Republic is definitely becoming one of these countries.

Mr. SMITH. Mr. Bolopion, you made I think a very constructive recommendation that we single out individuals and make it harder for them to travel, to, you know, isolate them. I would note parenthetically in 2004 I authored the Belarus Democracy Act, which, among its many other provisions, created a visa ban on Lukashenko and many of his henchmen.

And to our pleasant surprise, my pleasant surprise, the Europeans followed suit, and we pretty much have the same list of people who commit human rights atrocities who then can't travel to Europe or to the United States.

With regards to CAR, have our Government or the Europeans' or anyone done anything yet along these lines? Would it be hard to compile a list of individuals that should be so sanctioned? And it wouldn't just be visa bans. It would be, you know, trying to do, in a parallel way, what we do with foreign terrorist organizations. We go after their sources of funding, make it harder for them to do business, if you will. Your thoughts on that?

Mr. BOLOPION. Mr. Chairman, I think it is really something to look into in more detail. I don't believe any of these individuals have been put under sanction in any country right now. These sanctions are most effective when they are taken at the level of the U.N. Security Council, because certainly these individuals not only cannot travel or have bank accounts in the U.S., but they cannot travel or have bank accounts in any other countries.

And so some of the Seleka leaders have family or businesses in Chad, in Sudan, in Gulf countries, in places like that. So they have interests in foreign places. The reason why, talking to diplomats, I believe these type of sanctions have not been adopted yet is the lack of information that governments regret when it comes to the situation.

I believe that there is a lot of information out there now. We certainly have allowed—many of the individuals committing crimes are not even hiding very well. So if there is the political will to go after them, I think it can easily be done, and I believe that to be effective it should be done at the U.S. level, as well as the U.N. level. And the U.S. mission in New York can show leadership on this issue if it decides to.

Mr. SMITH. Yes, Mr. Jobbins.

Mr. JOBBINS. I think the only thing that I would add to that— I think that is something we all agree with—is also just to recognize the dissuasive power, not just of accountability but of communicating about accountability and making sure—just the notion that there is an attention to the commission of war crimes and other kinds of mechanisms, has a positive effect in dissuading future events.

And we have seen individual Seleka commanders be transferred because of outrage at some of the crimes that they have committed, and so we—you know, some messaging that accompanies that is something that would be very welcome.

Mr. SMITH. You know, because the NSA is probably reading my emails and yours, it does seem to be a matter of prioritization and taking that initiative to do it. We will follow up on that, and I thank you for that recommendation.

You know, you also made a recommendation that the ICC look into what is going on in the CAR. I recently chaired a hearing and wrote an op-ed for The Washington Post on Syria and the fact, in my opinion, that a regional or ad hoc tribunal might be far superior because of the focus, the buy-in from the local individuals.

And we had David Crane, the Chief Prosecutor for the Special Court for Sierra Leone, testify, and he is part of an accountability project vis-à -vis Syria right now, gathering information about atrocities, who, what, where, why—we know the why—and when. And, you know, the hope is that something like that can be set up.

Parenthetically, my concern with the ICC has been, and it certainly has a role to play, but they have had 18 indictments and one conviction, somebody from the DR Congo, who has been convicted and they are looking at three individuals with Boko Haram right now.

So your thoughts perhaps on a justice mechanism that might be different in the ICC. You know, they could do it, but I think they will go for one or two people, if that, and leave out the dozens that might also be, you know, held to account for their atrocities.

Mr. BOLOPION. Thank you, Mr. Chairman. This was not exactly a recommendation. The ICC has already declared that they were actively looking into the situation, so they are aware of it. We believe that they will be the appropriate place to judge people who are most responsible for the horrendous crimes that have been created there.

Now, you are exactly right that this will not be enough. They will not go after the lower-level commanders on the ground who are involved in some of these crimes. The types of mechanisms that we will require will have to be part of the discussion, and, frankly, could be part of what a U.N. peacekeeping mission would look like.

We have to keep in mind that whenever a U.N. peacekeeping mission deploys in the country it doesn't come with just military; it comes with a lot of civilians who are doing exactly this type of work and are trained to help people rebuild the justice system, try to make sure that minimum standards are in place. When people are arrested and charged, they can look into truth and reconciliation commissions, alongside this type of thing.

So we are just at the very beginning, but these are important questions that will need to be addressed.

Mr. SMITH. Bishop. Thank you.

Bishop NONGO-AZIAGBIA. In the advocacy mission, that the Central African civil society made to U.N. in the month of September, here in Washington in the month of September, one of the points we stressed, it was to fight against impunity. There are what my colleague used to say—the big fish can be looked after by the international penal court, and then they have to set up at the national level the judicial systems, which might take into consideration all those who have committed any abuses of any kind.

The BINUCA has received a political mandate with particular regard to justice, impunity, abuses. I hope they will get the necessary funding and the adequate personnel to look into this matter.

Mr. SMITH. Mr. Jobbins, you mentioned on point three of your four points, humanitarian response. There is a tremendous humanitarian need, and you point out that, as I noted before, the human and operational capacity exists in-country to begin meeting those needs, but there are significant funding shortfalls in order to respond.

Perhaps all three of you—and, Bishop, if you wouldn't mind providing us as detailed as possible an assessment of what those needs are, with as close to a price tag as you can put together, so we can advocate for—this subcommittee certainly has jurisdiction, and I can tell you that both myself and the ranking member want to ensure that—and the rest of the committee that those needs are being met.

I think it is appalling that 35,000 people that you take care of, and we are not helping—we are giving verbal support, but we are not giving tangible support. So in as precise a fashion as you can, to detail the needs, and the unmet need especially, so we can, as best we can, admonish and maybe even legislate, particularly through the appropriations process, sufficient funding to meet that need.

So if you could make that available to us, all three of you, I would say it would be very, very helpful.

Yes.

Mr. BOLOPION. Thank you, Mr. Chairman. I would say it is hard to put a price tag on it. I would say the new number one is for security. Humanitarian aid will not be delivered in the kind of villages we went to unless the roads are secured, for example. The civil society will not flourish. Many things will not happen as long as we have a few men with guns running entire areas.

Now, this of course has a price, and a U.N. peacekeeping mission has a price. I believe it would be a good investment. The solution of supporting an African Union mission would be probably a bit less costly in the short term, but I believe that in the longer term, if the country descends into chaos, it will have been a mistake to make that decision based on cost only.

On the humanitarian situation, all I can tell you is that according to the U.N. this is one of the worst humanitarian crises, and it is also one of the most underfunded. So the needs are huge, and governments are not contributing enough.

Finally, the Bishop pointed to something very important. BINUCA, the U.N. office there where I went to in Bangui, they were given with Resolution 2121 a very strong mandate, including to do human rights monitoring, exactly the type of things we do, but we are not there all the time, we go to a new few places.

The abuses that I described are horrendous, but we see only a very small window into what is really happening in the full country. The U.N. should have human rights monitors deployed throughout. They have a mandate to do that but not the resources yet.

Mr. SMITH. Thank you.

Mr. JOBBINS. From my end, I can—there are some numbers and some estimations that have been done by the U.N. Office for the Coordination of Humanitarian Affairs that brought together the different NGOs who are working and can give a full scientific estimate.

But from all of my conversations with our peers in the humanitarian community around town, our sense is that by far the medical supplies, food assistance, shelter, and support for IDPs, displaced people, are the three or four sorts of emergency life-saving assistance that are needed right away, and that there are many expert groups around town. And so I would defer to their assistance in compiling those numbers. I can send it along to you later.

And alongside that, of course, on the humanitarian side is the need to prevent violence and prevent further violence and integrate that into all of the work that we do.

Bishop NONGO-AZIAGBIA. The list might be long, very long, because presently most of the villages have been burned down. So the displaced people need to start new lives, build new houses, get furniture, the basic elements they need to start their lives. Their crops have been completely destroyed, so they have to start fresh. Where to get the crops, the seeds, that is another question. It will need some funding.

On health care, on education, the administration has been completely destroyed, so if we want the country to start, we have to redeploy the administration to rebuild the country. So we will deploy the civil servants, the judiciary members, and all that. We have to look at the offices. In that regard, the government will need some financial help.

The most important above all is the security, because you can't do any of that without security, and we can work with CRS to get you details of assistance. We are already working on needs.

Mr. SMITH. Thank you. And I look forward to working with all of you to get those detailed responses.

Without objection, a fact sheet by the United States Commission on International Religious Freedom entitled ''Increasing Sectarianism and Violence in the Central African Republic'' will be made a part of the record. And a letter from Chairman Royce to Secretary of State John Kerry dated November 7 will also be made a part of the record.

And I do have one final question, and that would be, you know, you point out, Bishop, that another important factor in this conflict is the presence of gold and diamonds, and the CAR Seleka militia groups are already in control of gold and diamond mining areas.

And I am wondering, because that can be a source of unbelievably tremendous subsidization for these terrible activities, is the international community responding to that? Has another blood diamonds situation emerged? And how effective are any of us being in focusing on that?

As we have done in the past, and there are mechanisms in place now, are they being utilized to ensure that none of those diamonds and none of that gold that is extracted by these killers, these terrorists, gets into New York, London, or anywhere else in the world?

Mr. BOLOPION. If I may on that, Mr. Chairman, we have not done any research on the exploitation of natural resources in the country. I think it is a great thing to look at.

Just a little anecdote from my trip there, I met with the security minister when I was in Bangui, Pastor Josue Binoua, who used to be a minister under the government of former President Bozize. He is in charge of the military and the police. He has 6,000 men under his control. By the way, only 110 weapons he told me.

But while I was with him, he was receiving a lot of phone calls on his cell phones trying to manage different crises. One of them he explained to me was that some, what he called Chinese businessmen, had just been arrested by his men at the airport trying to smuggle, out of the country, large quantities of gold.

And they were caught, arrested, and he was receiving phone calls from another minister from the Seleka, from the government, whom he did not name, but whom he said was threatening him, telling him, ''You need to release these guys, they are working with me. If you don't release them, you will find me on your way.'' So I think that tells you a lot about these dynamics.

Mr. SMITH. Can I ask you on that, is there any evidence, as we saw with Bashir in Khartoum, of Chinese complicity with the terrorists?

Mr. BOLOPION. I have absolutely no basis to say that the Chinese Government——

Mr. SMITH. Okay. Is anybody looking, do you know?

Mr. BOLOPION [continuing]. Would be involved in this in any way.

Bishop NONGO-AZIAGBIA. To the best of my knowledge, I would say that the Chinese presence in the Central African Republic is not on side of any rebel groups. They are there for their own business. And what has brought them to the Central African Republic, it is the mineral resources the country is having.

And just to give another anecdote like the first speaker has just given, it is at the airport, the police officer in charge came across someone who was probably carrying a huge amount of money in a European currency. It was far beyond what is allowed. And then he just made that clear to the passenger, he won't allow him to go across with his police formality.

That man picked his phone, talked to someone who happened to be the President. He passed on the phone to that police officer who refused to take it. A few minutes later on, the President presented himself at the airport, and then blaming that police officer who was just doing his job.

So that is where we are standing. The politicians are using all the means just to enrich themselves at the expense of the country.

Mr. SMITH. Thank you. Is there anything else any of you would like to add before we conclude today's hearing?

Mr. BOLOPION. Just to thank you, Mr. Chairman, for organizing this discussion. It is really heartening to hear this country being discussed in the U.S. Congress.

Mr. SMITH. Thank you.

Mr. JOBBINS. I would just add my voice as well to thank you all for your attention.

Bishop NONGO-AZIAGBIA. Thank you for this opportunity.

Mr. SMITH. I thank you for your extraordinary leadership, the insights you provided us, and look forward to working with you going forward.

The hearing is adjourned.

[Whereupon, at 12:33 p.m., the subcommittee was adjourned.]

APPENDIX

MATERIAL SUBMITTED FOR THE RECORD

SUBCOMMITTEE HEARING NOTICE
COMMITTEE ON FOREIGN AFFAIRS
U.S. HOUSE OF REPRESENTATIVES
WASHINGTON, DC 20515-6128

Subcommittee on Africa, Global Health, Global Human Rights, and International Organizations
Christopher H. Smith (R-NJ), Chairman

November 19, 2013

TO: MEMBERS OF THE COMMITTEE ON FOREIGN AFFAIRS

You are respectfully requested to attend an OPEN hearing of the Committee on Foreign Affairs, to be held by the Subcommittee on Africa, Global Health, Global Human Rights, and International Organizations in Room 2172 of the Rayburn House Office Building (and available live on the Committee website at www.foreignaffairs.house.gov):

DATE: Tuesday, November 19, 2013

TIME: 10:00 a.m.

SUBJECT: Crisis in the Central African Republic

WITNESSES: Panel I
The Honorable Robert P. Jackson
Principal Deputy Assistant Secretary
Bureau of African Affairs
U.S. Department of State

Panel II
The Most Reverend Nestor-Désiré Nongo-Aziagbia
Roman Catholic Bishop of Bossangoa, Central African Republic

Mr. Mike Jobbins
Senior Programme Manager, Africa
Search for Common Ground

Mr. Philippe Bolopion
United Nations Director
Human Rights Watch

By Direction of the Chairman

The Committee on Foreign Affairs seeks to make its facilities accessible to persons with disabilities. If you are in need of special accommodations, please call 202/225-5021 at least four business days in advance of the event, whenever practicable. Questions with regard to special accommodations in general (including availability of Committee materials in alternative formats and assistive listening devices) may be directed to the Committee.

COMMITTEE ON FOREIGN AFFAIRS

MINUTES OF SUBCOMMITTEE ON *Africa, Global Health, Global Human Rights, and International Organizations* HEARING

Day___*Tuesday*___Date_*November 19, 2013*___Room_*2172 Rayburn HOB*___

Starting Time___*10:00 a.m.*___Ending Time ,_*12:33 p.m.*___

Recesses [___*0*___] (____to ____) (____to ____) (____to ____) (____to ____) (____to ____) (____to ____)

Presiding Member(s)

Rep. Chris Smith

Check all of the following that apply:

Open Session ☑   Electronically Recorded (taped) ☑
Executive (closed) Session ☐   Stenographic Record ☑
Televised ☑

TITLE OF HEARING:

Crisis in the Central African Republic

SUBCOMMITTEE MEMBERS PRESENT:

Rep. Meadows, Rep. Marino, Rep. Bass, Rep. Cicilline

NON-SUBCOMMITTEE MEMBERS PRESENT: *(Mark with an * if they are not members of full committee.)*

Rep. Royce

HEARING WITNESSES: Same as meeting notice attached? Yes ☑ No ☐
(If "no", please list below and include title, agency, department, or organization.)

STATEMENTS FOR THE RECORD: *(List any statements submitted for the record.)*

Factsheet from the US Commission on International Religious Freedom
Letter from Rep. Royce to Sec. Kerry

TIME SCHEDULED TO RECONVENE _____
or
TIME ADJOURNED ___*12:33 p.m.*___

Gregory B. Simpkins
Subcommittee Staff Director

MATERIAL SUBMITTED FOR THE RECORD BY THE HONORABLE CHRISTOPHER H. SMITH, A REPRESENTATIVE IN CONGRESS FROM THE STATE OF NEW JERSEY, AND CHAIRMAN, SUBCOMMITTEE ON AFRICA, GLOBAL HEALTH, GLOBAL HUMAN RIGHTS, AND INTERNATIONAL ORGANIZATIONS

UNITED STATES COMMISSION ON INTERNATIONAL RELIGIOUS FREEDOM

Increasing Sectarianism and Violence in the Central African Republic

The Central African Republic (CAR) has a long history of political strife that frequently has led to coups and human rights abuses. Yet the current chaos and fighting following the March 2013 coup against former President Francoise Bozizé is uniquely dangerous, as it increasingly is centered around religious identity and risks pulling the country into an intractable Muslim-Christian conflict. If these forces are not contained, severe human rights abuses are expected to be increasingly perpetrated along religious and ethnic lines. The UN Special Adviser on the Prevention of Genocide, Adama Dieng, noted these very concerns when he warned recently that the CAR may spiral into genocide. In addition, the growing conflict and lawlessness could turn the CAR into a failed state vulnerable to terrorist groups from either East or West Africa looking to expand their operations.

Background

Fighting began in December 2012 when a coalition of armed rebels, the Séléka, advanced on the CAR capital, Bangui, in response to the government's failure to implement provisions of the 2007 and 2011 peace accords to pay former rebel fighters and integrate them into the army. The Séléka (Sango for coalition) is an alliance of fighters from at least four armed rebel groups that have been operating in the northern part of the country since 2003: the Convention of Patriots for Justice and Peace, the Convention of Patriots of Salvation and Kodro, the Democratic Front of the Central African People, and the Union of Democratic Forces for Unity. The fighters are Muslims from CAR's almost universally Muslim Vakaga region in the northeast of the country, a large number of foreign fighters from Chad and Sudan, and some of former President Bozizé guards and soldiers. At the beginning of the rebellion, the Séléka were estimated to number around 5,000, but Amnesty International now reports estimates of up to 20,000 soldiers. The rebellion was led by Michel Djotodia, a Muslim from the Vakaga region and a former Ministry of Planning official and Consulate Council in Nyala, South Darfur.

By the time the fighters reached the outskirts of the capital Bangui in December 2012 they controlled two-thirds of the country, including the major city of Bambari and the diamond mining town of Bria. Before the Séléka could take Bangui, neighboring countries politically intervened to end the fighting. The regional intervention by Chad and the Economic Community of Central African States (ECCAS) led to the signing on January 11, 2013 of the Libreville Agreement.

The short-lived Libreville Agreement upheld the 2003 constitution and set up a three year power-sharing Government of National Unity that would end with presidential elections in 2016. Per the Agreement, the GNU was to be led by President Bozizé through 2016 and a presidentially-appointed Prime Minister with full executive powers who would come from the opposition. The

National Assembly would be dissolved and replaced with newly elected representatives within 12 months.

Bozizé failed to implement the Libreville Agreement, which led the Séléka to once again take up arms. On March 24, 2013 the Séléka captured the capital Bangui and deposed Bozizé. Djotodia proclaimed himself President and Minister of Defense; appointed opposition party leader Nicolas Tiangaye Prime Minister; suspended the Constitution; dissolved the National Assembly, the Constitutional Court and the Government of National Unity; and appointed a new government, composed of representatives from Séléka, opposition parties, civil society, and one Bozizé ally.

In response to these new developments, Chad organized two summits of African states and CAR leaders on April 3 and 18 culminating in the N'Djamena Declaration and the N'Djamena Summit Road Map. The new CAR transitional government was recognized, a new 18 month transitional period led by a National Transition Council was tasked to draft a new constitution and prepare for new elections, and a new constitutional court was agreed upon. Djotodia was formally sworn in as interim president on August 18, marking the beginning of the 18-month transition period.

Current human rights situation in the Central African Republic

The Séléka are responsible for a breakdown in the overall human rights and rule of law environment in the CAR. The transitional government remains very weak and is absent outside of Bangui, as are rule of law institutions such as the police or judiciary and government service providers. Séléka fighters freely roam the country. Former special representative of the UN Secretary-General to the CAR, Margaret Aderinsola Vogt, told the Security Council in May that the country had plunged into a "state of anarchy."

There are continuous reports of killings, torture, arbitrary detention, gender-based violence, and enforced disappearances by the Séléka. Séléka fighters also loot property and food from civilians, churches, international nongovernmental organizations (NGOs), and UN agencies; recruit and use child soldiers; and engage in sexual violence. International charities report having to pay Séléka rebels to prevent being robbed. The human rights situation has worsened since June, following a breakdown in Séléka cohesion, and again since September with the formation of anti-Séléka militias.

Since March, the four associated groups and other parties comprising the Séléka a have become increasingly disorganized, with the various factions and fighters increasingly difficult to control. Séléka members repeatedly have been involved in gross human rights abuses. The UN reports that Séléka leaders can access only areas controlled by men loyal to them, as different factions do not recognize leaders from other groups. While Djotodia signed a presidential decree in September disbanding the Séléka, the rebels continue to operate and commit gross human rights abuses.

Current religious freedom violations

The CAR is a majority Christian country. Eighty five percent of its citizens are identified as Lutheran, Catholic, Protestant, or Evangelical. The remaining 15 percent are Sunni Muslim. The Muslim population can be found in the Vakaga district, a poor and remote area in the north-east of CAR located at the borders with Chad and Sudan where Arabic is the primary language.

According to recent State Department International Religious Freedom reports, prior to the 2012-2013 rebellion and subsequent coup, Muslims faced consistent social discrimination and Muslim citizens were labelled "foreigners." Low-level bureaucrats impeded access to services like citizenship documentation. Muslim-owned shops frequently were vandalized and, in some cases, vigilantes subjected Muslims to harassment, beatings, and detention. There also were reports of isolated clashes between Muslim nomadic groups and Christian or non-Muslim farmers and between Muslim traders and others.

In the CAR's current lawless environment, a number of identifiable religious freedom violations have occurred. The United Nations, International Crisis Group, Human Rights Watch, Amnesty International, Christian religious leaders, and humanitarian organizations all report that the Séléka attack priests, pastors, nuns, church buildings, and other Christian institutions. Séléka soldiers are reported to have beaten Catholic priests Abbé Philippe Greballe and Abbé Alain Banganzi, and nuns are threatened with rape. The Brethren church in Bangui's Cité Jean XXIII quarter was shelled during a worship service on April 14, killing or seriously injuring a number of people, including children. The Catholic Church of Basse Kotto Prefecture and the Mobaye Catholic Church were looted and damaged in late January and early February 2013, respectively. On April 13-14, clashes along religious lines occurred between Séléka elements and the population of Ouango and Boy-Rabe in Bangui, killing and displacing large numbers of civilians.

Additionally, during their advances toward Bangui in December 2012 and March 2013, the Séléka targeted predominantly Christian neighborhoods and businesses were targeted for destruction. Séléka fighters in different villages, such as Bambari, Bangui, Boali, and Markounda, looted churches but not mosques. In other villages, the Séléka protected Muslim residents while Christian residents were killed or raped and their properties were destroyed and looted. Amnesty International and Catholic leaders report that in some Séléka-controlled areas, non-Muslims are prohibited from selling foods not eaten by CAR Muslims, including pork, bushmeat and caterpillars.

Concerns for the future

The rise of the almost universally Muslim Séléka and CAR's first Muslim leader has increased fear and confusion among CAR's Christian population. Neighboring countries are also increasingly concerned about CAR's internal religious tensions and rising religious fundamentalism. The UN Assistant Secretary-General for Human Rights has warned that "The conflict in the Central African Republic should not remain forgotten for three main reasons: conflict will continue to impose suffering on large numbers of people, it will deepen the religious and ethnic divide, and it may destabilize the wider region." The International Crisis Group reports that in online forums, some CAR citizens and members of the diaspora have encouraged the population to take up arms and systematically retaliate against any and all Muslims.

These fears are based on the facts that large percentages of Séléka soldiers are from Chad and Sudan; wounded Séléka soldiers have been flown by military aircraft to Sudan and Saudi Arabia for treatment; Séléka leaders have visited Qatar; Djotodia has strengthened ties with Morocco and Sudan; and most importantly, a rumor that in the April 2012, Djotodia wrote to the Organization of Islamic Conference (OIC) asking for monetary and material support, and in return, the Séléka would implement Islamic law across the CAR and try to do likewise in Chad. Djotodia has since denied writing this letter and reaffirmed that CAR will remain a secular state.

In response to the Séléka attacks, a number of militias have formed to fight back. Known as the anti-balaka (Sango for anti-machete), these disparate groups can be characterized as local self-defense militias who are Christian, pro-Christian militias, or militias made up of Christian Bozizé supporters. The various anti-balaka militias, depending on the situation, attack the Séléka, individual Muslims, and/or Muslim villages.

For example, on September 6, anti-balaka fighters killed or captured 20 Séléka fighters and targeted Muslim homes in Benzambé. Three days later, on September 9, the anti-balaka attacked a Muslim neighborhood in Bouca, killing three people and burning 150 homes belonging to Muslims. In response, Séléka fighters that same day in Bouca killed 10 Christians and burned down 300 homes belonging to Christians. A Séléka commander also accused a humanitarian worker of assisting the anti-balaka and executed him. In early October, Séléka and anti-balaka clashes again broke out. On October 7, anti-balaka and Séléka engaged in battle in Gaga village, before the anti-balaka attacked Muslim civilians. Two days later, the Séléka retaliated in Gaga, targeting Christians. Doctors Without Borders reports that more than 100 people died in this fighting. Anti-balaka and Séléka attacks and counter-attacks also occurred on October 12 in Bomboro and on October 26 in Bouar, killing dozens.

The increase of fighting between the Séléka and the anti-balaka falls along religious lines, and is so viewed by CAR's many citizens. French UN Ambassador Gerard Araud said on November 1, "More and more you have inter-sectarian violence because the Séléka targeted the churches and the Christians, so now the Christians have created self-defense militias and they are retaliating against the Muslims." The BBC reports that displaced residents of the Bozizé's hometown of Bossangoa have fled to their co-religionists and that the town is split in half into Muslim-Christian areas. Displaced Christian Bossangoa residents also reported to the BBC that they fear if they leave their refuge in the Christian Mission that the Séléka fighters will identify them as Christian and detain, beat, shoot or kill them. Muslim residents report carrying weapons with them at all times. Amnesty International and Doctors Without Borders report that on September 29, Séléka soldiers executed two Christians south of Bossangoa and on October 4, anti-Balaka separated eight Muslims from a group of travelers between Bangui and Bossangoa and shot them.

U.S. government and the international community response

The United Nations, AU, ECCAS, and France have led the international response to the crisis in the Central African Republic. The African Union plans to deploy a 3,600-member peacekeeping mission, the International Support Mission in the Central African Republic (MISCA), in the country. This force would incorporate ECCAS soldiers already on the ground, but will not be fully operational before 2014. The Security Council on October 10 adopted a resolution asking UN Secretary-General Ban Ki-moon to outline "detailed options for international support to MISCA, including the possible option of a transformation of MISCA into a United Nations peacekeeping operation, subject to appropriate conditions on the ground." In October, the Security Council approved a plan by the Secretary General to send 250 military personnel to Bangui plus 560 troops to be deployed outside the capital where there is a UN presence. France plans to have a small force of 700 soldiers in Bangui by the end of the year, but only to secure the airport and its local interests.

The U.S. government supports UN, AU, and ECCAS efforts to bring stability to the CAR; condemns the ongoing gross human rights abuses and insecurity; calls for the transitional government to move toward elections in 2015 and adopt a new constitution to bring democracy to the country; and funds humanitarian assistance operations in and outside of CAR. The U.S. government condemned the Séléka's seizure of power in March, followed by Djotodia's self-appointment as president, and his decisions to end the transitional governance structures implemented by the Libreville Agreement. It primarily works with the Prime Minister. The U.S. government closed its Embassy in Bangui in December 2012 for security reasons and the Embassy remains closed. A Senior Advisor is in place, however, to address the crisis.

MATERIAL SUBMITTED FOR THE RECORD BY THE HONORABLE EDWARD R. ROYCE, A REPRESENTATIVE IN CONGRESS FROM THE STATE OF CALIFORNIA, AND CHAIRMAN, COMMITTEE ON FOREIGN AFFAIRS

EDWARD R. ROYCE, CALIFORNIA
CHAIRMAN

CHRISTOPHER H. SMITH, NEW JERSEY
ILEANA ROS-LEHTINEN, FLORIDA
DANA ROHRABACHER, CALIFORNIA
STEVE CHABOT, OHIO
JOE WILSON, SOUTH CAROLINA
MICHAEL T. McCAUL, TEXAS
TED POE, TEXAS
MATT SALMON, ARIZONA
TOM MARINO, PENNSYLVANIA
JEFF DUNCAN, SOUTH CAROLINA
ADAM KINZINGER, ILLINOIS
MO BROOKS, ALABAMA
TOM COTTON, ARKANSAS
PAUL COOK, CALIFORNIA
GEORGE HOLDING, NORTH CAROLINA
RANDY K. WEBER SR., TEXAS
SCOTT PERRY, PENNSYLVANIA
STEVE STOCKMAN, TEXAS
RON DESANTIS, FLORIDA
TREY RADEL, FLORIDA
DOUG COLLINS, GEORGIA
MARK MEADOWS, NORTH CAROLINA
TED S. YOHO, FLORIDA
LUKE MESSER, INDIANA

AMY PORTER
CHIEF OF STAFF

THOMAS SHEEHY
STAFF DIRECTOR

ELIOT L. ENGEL, NEW YORK
RANKING DEMOCRATIC MEMBER

ENI F.H. FALEOMAVAEGA, AMERICAN SAMOA
BRAD SHERMAN, CALIFORNIA
GREGORY W. MEEKS, NEW YORK
ALBIO SIRES, NEW JERSEY
GERALD E. CONNOLLY, VIRGINIA
THEODORE E. DEUTCH, FLORIDA
BRIAN HIGGINS, NEW YORK
KAREN BASS, CALIFORNIA
WILLIAM KEATING, MASSACHUSETTS
DAVID CICILLINE, RHODE ISLAND
ALAN GRAYSON, FLORIDA
JUAN VARGAS, CALIFORNIA
BRADLEY S. SCHNEIDER, ILLINOIS
JOSEPH P. KENNEDY III, MASSACHUSETTS
AMI BERA, CALIFORNIA
ALAN S. LOWENTHAL, CALIFORNIA
GRACE MENG, NEW YORK
LOIS FRANKEL, FLORIDA
TULSI GABBARD, HAWAII
JOAQUIN CASTRO, TEXAS

JASON STEINBAUM
DEMOCRATIC STAFF DIRECTOR

One Hundred Thirteenth Congress
U.S. House of Representatives
Committee on Foreign Affairs
2170 Rayburn House Office Building
Washington, DC 20515
www.foreignaffairs.house.gov

November 7, 2013

The Honorable John F. Kerry
Secretary of State
U.S. Department of State
2201 C Street, N.W.
Washington, DC 20520

Dear Mr. Secretary:

I am writing to express my concern with the abysmal state of affairs in the Central African Republic (C.A.R.) and urge meaningful and practical engagement by the State Department.

Since Seleka rebels seized Bangui, forcibly ousting President Francois Bozize and installing a rebel commander to fill the role, C.A.R. has spiraled into a state of lawlessness. Reports indicate that several hundred thousand civilians have been displaced internally or fled to neighboring countries. With no government security forces in place, the rebels operate without restraint, indiscriminately killing, looting, and torturing innocent civilians. Prime Minster Nicolas Tiangaye, the only current C.A.R. official recognized as a legitimate leader by the international community, described his own country as "anarchy, a nonstate" and explained that the rebels "are sowing terrorism." His comments are particularly disturbing given the pattern of ethno-religious violence that has emerged in parts of the country.

The United States has a national security interest in seeing that C.A.R. regains a semblance of order and stability. C.A.R. shares borders with six countries, some which have received significant U.S. assistance, elevating its regional importance. These countries are contending with an influx of refugees from C.A.R and the potential for heightened inter-communal tensions as religious and identity fault-lines deepen as a consequence. The Ugandan-led, African Union military operation to counter the Lord's Resistance Army, which receives U.S. government logistical and advisory support, operates in C.A.R.'s southwest and was halted for several months this year due to C.A.R.'s insecurity and political uncertainty. Additionally, with no semblance of the rule of law, the situation in the country lends itself to transnational criminal activity, such as wildlife trafficking and illicit resource extraction, both of which the State Department has attempted to curtail on the continent.

The Honorable John F. Kerry
November 7, 2013
Page 2

I understand that the U.N. Security Council has taken certain actions regarding the situation in C.A.R. and that the State Department is giving consideration to providing support to the African Union-led International Support Mission to the Central African Republic (MISCA). I urge you to remain substantively engaged with these international efforts, and to keep the Committee fully informed as you evaluate options to provide bilateral and/or multilateral support to this mission.

The appalling security and humanitarian conditions in C.A.R. warrant substantive international engagement. With U.S. national security interests at stake, I look forward to working with you in developing concentrate steps to help address instability in the Central African Republic.

Sincerely,

EDWARD R. ROYCE
Chairman